PRIESTHOOD
IN A TIME OF CRISIS

"Rossetti's important new study brings to light the truth that the overwhelming majority of priests find joy and fulfillment in their call from God. It will help the laity to understand the tremendous gift and sometimes challenging life of the priest today, and ought to guide formation programs for priests throughout the country."

Msgr. Robert Panke
Pastor, Saint John Neumann Catholic Church
Gaithersburg, Maryland

"Both hopeful and challenging, *Priesthood in a Time of Crisis* helps to overturn the persistent stereotype of priests as disgruntled and depressed. From a data-driven perspective, Msgr. Stephen Rossetti shows that priests are broadly happy with their vocation, convinced that their life is deeply meaningful, and committed to celibacy. Rossetti uncovers the key indicators of a priest's spiritual and psychological well-being, including those that are most likely to stifle the initial zeal and enthusiasm for the priestly vocation. This book is enormously helpful and encouraging for priests and for those involved in priestly formation and indeed for all Catholics who love their priests and wish to support them with their prayers, assistance, and affection."

Fr. Carter Griffin
Rector, Saint John Paul II Seminary
Washington, DC

"Rossetti's new book points to the truth that one can find great joy in following the call of Jesus Christ into the priestly vocation. Rossetti also provides a clear look at the foundational components of wellness and thriving: good connection to community, strong habits of prayer, and integration of pastoral charity."

Fr. James Gallagher, CSC
Superior and rector, Moreau Seminary
Notre Dame, Indiana

"I urge every vocation director, seminary formator, and bishop to read this book. Rossetti offers not only valuable insight on the health of today's priesthood and the direct correlation to a strong spiritual life, but also wise, practical suggestions for ensuring priests are supported in contemporary American culture, which is both challenging and rewarding."

Rosemary C. Sullivan
Executive Director
National Conference of Diocesan Vocation Directors

PRIESTHOOD
IN A TIME OF CRISIS

*A New Study of the Psychological
and Spiritual Health of Priests*

MSGR. STEPHEN J. ROSSETTI

AVE MARIA PRESS AVE Notre Dame, Indiana

Nihil obstat: Rev. Msgr. Charles Pope
            Censor deputatus
            January 6, 2023

Imprimatur: Very Rev. George E. Stuart, JCD
            Episcopal Vicar for Canonical Services
            Roman Catholic Archdiocese of Washington
            January 9, 2023

Founded in 1865, Ave Maria Press is a ministry of the United States Province of Holy Cross.

www.avemariapress.com

Paperback: ISBN-13 978-1-64680-208-1

E-book: ISBN-13 978-1-64680-209-8

Cover image © Getty Images.

Cover and text design by Andy Wagoner.

Printed and bound in the United States of America.

CONTENTS

ILLUSTRATIONS

INTRODUCTION

It has been a rough couple of decades for the Catholic faithful in the United States in general and, in particular, for Catholic priests. The sexual abuse crisis seemingly will never end. Revelations about it started in earnest in the 1990s and have only gotten worse. The drubbing of the Catholic leadership and the priests in the US media and beyond has been intense and relentless.

This of course has been followed by the COVID-19 pandemic, which has lasted more than two years at this writing. The pandemic and subsequent restrictions have affected nearly everyone around the globe at a personal level. Loved ones have died; businesses have shuttered; mask, social distancing, and vaccination mandates have proliferated. Not surprisingly, rates of depression and anxiety have spiked across populations. Isolation and fear prevail. Uncertainty and misinformation confuse and confound.

Priests have not been immune to the impact of the COVID-19 pandemic. Priests have been cut off from their people, often celebrating Mass alone in their chapels. For more than a few, the isolation has been painful. Their ministries have been crippled and their emotional contact largely curtailed. As one priest wrote in the comments section of the survey behind this current study: "I think that everyone agrees that there are two ongoing problems these days, (1) The scandals among some of the ordained brothers and (2) The emotionally killing effects of this endless pandemic on social and pastoral life."

There are many who erroneously assert that priests today suffer from low morale. Given all that has happened, it would not be irrational to assume so. For example, a 2020 article in a well-known Catholic magazine reported, "The vast majority of our priests are deeply demoralized." The author offered no statistics but based the credibility of his statement on his "probably knowing more priests in the country than anyone else."[1]

It is widely assumed that priests are lonely and unhappy. One can easily find and interview a priest who will say so. Likewise, priests' mental health is believed to be poor, and many are assumed to suffer from psychological and sexual problems. Some media have given the impression that sexual abuse is rampant among the clergy, likely because of their supposed dysfunctional lifestyles and psychological deficits.

Certainly, there are cases of priests who suffer from psychological disorders. As a priest and psychologist, I have spent thirty years ministering to such priests. There also are priests who are lonely and unhappy. Every day, I connect and minister to some who are. There are priests contemplating leaving the priesthood. A neighboring diocese just lost some young priests who resigned. But are these things the norm? Are the "vast majority" of priests demoralized and unhappy? It is dangerous to use inductive logic, making broad generalizations from a few cases.

I do not fault the media. Media accounts are good at raising important issues. How much progress would society in general, and the Church in particular, have made without such public pressure? But the media are not always good at presenting a balanced perspective of complex issues. The more sensational and shocking a story, the more it sells. One sure-fire story that captures public attention is a priest gone awry. It readily grabs attention.

Many articles on priestly happiness in secular magazines and at popular online sites characterize the state of priesthood in negative ways. I have read accounts of priestly despair and burnout.

Articles frequently assert that priests are dispirited. The "data" feeding such stories often come from individual cases of priests making the news or limited interviews of a few.

It is the responsibility of academics and researchers to take a deeper look. We are bound to present a more thorough, data-based perspective. The Church cannot effectively face its challenges without having an accurate understanding of the true nature of its problems. A doctor cannot apply a healing remedy without a correct diagnosis.

Herein lies a modest contribution to such research. I have endeavored to be as transparent with the data as possible so the reader can follow in some detail how I arrived at certain insights and conclusions. The reader is free to challenge the interpretation of the data.

A researcher is a slave to the data. While I have some latitude in interpreting them, the data are the data. At times, when I ran the numbers, I would hold my breath and say a little prayer. First, of course, I was hoping the results would be statistically significant. A study cannot conclude much when the data are not significant in a statistical sense. But more than that, I was hoping the data would paint an accurate picture of priesthood today.

The results exceeded my expectations. Not only were they statistically significant to a high degree, but they also painted a coherent picture of priesthood today. These results give us some initial insights into why priests are who they are. The data help tell us what makes a priest—who he is both psychologically and spiritually. They help us understand those who are coping well with the life and ministry of a celibate priest and those who are not.

The study provided an additional benefit. Having done similar studies in 2004 and 2009, I could compare the state of priests in the United States in 2021 with previous priestly cohorts. We can thus come to some initial longitudinal conclusions about priestly health and happiness over time. Are priests as a group getting happier or more miserable? Are they getting psychologically stronger or less so? Are such factors as priestly unity and support for their bishops becoming stronger or weaker?

But there is one contribution of this study that might outweigh the rest. I gathered these survey data primarily from December 2020 through February 2021, in the midst of the COVID-19 pandemic. At the time of the survey, the pandemic had been in full force for many months with all of its emotional and spiritual trauma. Initial secular studies demonstrated that the pandemic was taking a serious toll on the psychological health and wellness of Americans. This study looks at its effects on priests.

The survey also coincided with the gradual unfolding of the child sexual abuse crisis in the Catholic Church in the United States. Most notably, the data were gathered in the wake of several national eruptions of reporting in sex abuse scandals in the Church, such as the August 2018 release of the Pennsylvania grand jury report and the 2018 revelations of the scandal surrounding former cardinal Theodore McCarrick. The national abuse crisis figured prominently in the media for many months after the initial reporting. In an effort to confront the crisis, several states enacted "look back" legislation that allowed civil suits against the Church for old cases that formerly were outside of the statute of limitations. The resulting flood of lawsuits and the concomitant media storm kept the sexual abuse crisis in a prominent place in national news cycles until the pandemic largely eclipsed other news stories in early 2020. For priests, this was a very long and painful period.

The timing of this survey gives us a unique view of priesthood as affected by two major crises. It has been said that a person is best and most surely known in a crisis and under pressure. This has been a time of great pressure on priests. This study will give us a glimpse into the effects of these crises on priests and how priests are holding up. It will tell us a lot about Catholic priests ministering in the Church today.

In the course of this study, especially when reading the participants' written comments at the end of their surveys, I was often encouraged and, at times, edified. Sometimes, I grimaced at the pain and hurt in the voice of a priest. Almost universally, whether the priests were happy or not, I admired their self-sacrificing dedication to helping the People of God. I finish my thirty years of research into priesthood with this study. I have been richly blessed.

1

SUMMARY OF FINDINGS

This book presents the findings of survey research completed in 2021 of 1,962 priests from twenty-five dioceses across the United States. Those findings are supplemented by data from my previous research completed in 2009 of 2,482 priests from twenty-three dioceses and also my study in 2004 of 1,242 priests from sixteen dioceses. These research studies all focused on the psychological and spiritual wellness and happiness of Catholic priests in the United States.

These large-scale studies offer a unique glimpse into the psychological and spiritual state of our priests. The standard psychological tests included in the surveys allowed me to compare the mental health of priests to norm samples of the laity. Using modern statistical techniques enabled me to identify and probe those factors that make a happy and well priest.

In addition, since this was the third in a series of studies over seventeen years, the findings give us some longitudinal research information; that is, we can track changes in these issues over time. Moreover, since this most recent 2021 study was completed during the pandemic, we can compare these findings with those of previous studies and measure effects of the pandemic. Also, since the research occurred in the wake of another round of child sexual abuse scandals, we can look at the impact of the scandals on the priesthood. Thus this latest research study can investigate in some detail the effects of these two crises on the priesthood.

PRIESTHOOD AND HAPPINESS

This 2021 study of priests in the wake of the pandemic and child sexual abuse crisis found that the previously reported high rates of priestly happiness remained steady for the three studies: 2004, 2009, and 2021. Ninety percent or more of priests indicate they strongly agree or agree with the statement, "Overall, I am happy as a priest." For some years now, a number of other studies, both religious and secular, have corroborated these high rates of priestly happiness. As the Center for Applied Research in the Apostolate (CARA) concluded in 2014: "Priests are generally very happy with their lives and ministry. There is no overarching morale problem in the priesthood."[1]

Happiness levels of Americans reportedly took a nosedive in the midst of the pandemic. One study found that Americans who self-identified as "very happy" dropped sharply from 31% in 2018 to 19% in 2021. The Great Resignation of Americans during the pandemic might be a symptom of that sharp drop in happiness. However, there was no similar drop in self-reported priestly happiness levels, which remained above 90%.

One important contributor to these happiness levels among priests is their high satisfaction with ministry. They scored in the top quarter of Americans in satisfaction with their work. Priests like their work; they feel they are making a difference; and they confirm that they are happy to have chosen to be a priest.

Priestly happiness levels actually appear to be rising over the past few decades. Both Dean Hoge of the Catholic University of America and a recent CARA study also reported this phenomenon. There appeared to be a slight dip in priestly happiness in the wake of the 2002 sexual abuse crisis. However, in subsequent years, the percentage of priests reporting to be very happy rose to new heights.

One possible reason for rising happiness levels is the aging of the presbyterate. Older priests tend to report higher levels of happiness. Another possible reason is the increasing adherence to a more traditional theology by younger priests. Individuals who are more traditional are noted to report often higher satisfaction levels. However, this is partially offset by the challenges of being newly ordained.

In this study, priests born in Africa, India, Hispanic nations, and Southeast Asia reported higher levels of happiness than those born in the United States. This suggests that their welcome and integration into the Catholic Church in the United States is, on the whole, going well.

In the comments section at the end of the survey, the most often written statement by the priest-respondents was, "I love being a priest."

UNHAPPY PRIESTS

Six percent of the priest-respondents reported that they were "unsure" or "strongly disagree/disagree" with the statement, "Overall, I am happy as a priest." This study investigated some of the factors that might help us to understand unhappy priests a bit better.

The strongest predictors of what makes an unhappy priest were internal factors. Those who did not report positive self-esteem and/or reported a lack of inner peace were very likely to state that they were unhappy as a priest. The correlation of unhappiness with a lack of inner peace was a high $r = .61$ and with a lack of self-esteem was similarly strong, $r = .45$. (A strong positive correlation means that as one variable increases or decreases, the other variable does the same. While this does not of itself prove a causal relationship, it does suggest an important relationship between the variables that may be causal.) Happiness is an inside job, as is sometimes said. If a priest is unhappy, he might first look at his own internal sense of self.

The next strongest predictor of unhappiness was loneliness. Respondents who did not report having close priest or lay friends were much less likely to report being happy. Similarly, those who reported being lonely were much less likely to report being happy. Connections to others are critical for satisfaction with life for all people, including priests. Happiness rates for lonely priests without friends dropped approximately in half.

In today's culture, the seminary cannot assume that candidates for the priesthood have the experience and skills to develop nurturing relationships. If I could add one course to the seminary today, it would be a practical course in building relationships.

Priesthood is intrinsically connected to the spiritual life. There were few priests who reported not having a relationship with God. But those lacking that relationship were much less likely to be happy. The happiness rates for them declined more than half. Similarly, priests who reported a minimum of daily prayer were also much less likely to report being happy. Nurturing a spiritual life is important in sustaining the well-being of a priest.

An important finding was the connection between priests and their bishop. This 2021 study affirmed the findings of the 2009 study in demonstrating statistically just how strongly not having a good relationship with one's bishop influences a priest's happiness. The happiness levels of priests plummet when they do not have a positive connection to their bishop. The most frequent negative comments on the survey concerned the bishop or chancery.

This suggests that some unhappy priests focus their unhappiness on their leaders.

MENTAL HEALTH OF PRIESTS TODAY

The sexual abuse crisis has highlighted the importance of mental health in priests. It is currently common for dioceses to do some psychological screening for those applying to the priesthood. I am not aware of any diocese that does not have some form of such screening.

The overall level of mental health among priests remains stable in the midst of the two ongoing crises, and similar to the mental health of others in the general population as measured by a common psychological test, the Brief Symptom Inventory 18 (BSI-18). The pre-pandemic-level scores of mental health among priests were also similar to those of the general population.

However, in the midst of the pandemic, the rates of depression among priests nearly doubled, from 7.5% to 14.5%, and the rates of anxiety increased by 50%, from 6.4% to 9.3%. While this increase is a cause for concern, it is much less than the increase for the general population, which rose fourfold for both. Priests, in the midst of the pandemic, tested as more psychologically resilient than did their fellow Americans.

Rates of suicidal ideation among priests are very low. Priests who suffer from negative inner states of depression, anxiety, and burnout are at increased risk for suicidal ideation. It appears that having Christian beliefs does not stop one from having suicidal ideation but may have a positive effect on reducing suicidal attempts.

The rate of burnout among priests as a whole is relatively low. This does not mean they are not overworked or stretched thin; many are. The number of priests in the United States today dropped from 59,192 in 1970 to 35,513 in 2020. Over the same time period, the total Catholic population rose from 54.1 million to 72.4 million, placing more demands on our priests than ever before. But there is a difference between having too much work and being burned out. A number of personal factors sustain priests: they like their ministries; they have good friends; they have a strong spiritual life. Such factors promote health and tend to deter burnout.

Also, feeling competent to assist others in a crisis is important in helping priests to successfully weather a crisis themselves and to avert burning out. The large majority (80%) feel competent to assist others suffering from trauma. Given the rising level of terrorism and violence in our society and the world at large, I recommend that dioceses regularly train their priests and people in dealing with trauma, crises, and violence.

This study compared psychologically distressed priests with healthier priests, as measured by the BSI-18. The majority of psychologically distressed priests said they were very lonely compared with few of the healthy group. When priests get depressed, one of the strongest symptoms of their depression is loneliness. It is a strong marker of a priest at risk for depression.

There is a clear connection between the psychological and spiritual health of priests. The majority of psychologically healthy priests (79%) endorsed the statement "the Eucharist is the center of my life" versus much less (49%) of the psychologically distressed group. Similarly, the overall mental health of a priest is significantly correlated with his relationship to God ($r = .31$). Thus, as the priest's spirituality improves, so does his mental health.

Priests who suffered trauma in childhood tend to be more vulnerable to burnout. They are less likely to be happy in priesthood, less likely to be happy with self, and more likely to suffer from anxiety or depression as an adult. These factors highlight the importance of screening before ordination. About one-fifth of priests say that they were traumatized or suffered psychologically in childhood. It is important for these individuals to have found some healing in order to have a successful ministry.

Priests in the first ten years of ordination were somewhat more likely to suffer from anxiety, depression, and/or burnout. The Church should not underestimate the personal challenges of adjusting to the demanding ministry of a priest. This affirms the need for support programs for the newly ordained, which many dioceses have.

Internal psychological distress, as measured by depression and anxiety, is a very strong predictor of low morale and thoughts of leaving the ministry. It is critical for dioceses and religious orders to identify and assist priests who are suffering from internal distress, especially depression and anxiety. There is a very strong likelihood that such priests are isolated, unhappy, living a degraded spiritual life, and perhaps even thinking of leaving the ministry.

It is a positive sign that 39% of priest-respondents say they have been in counseling. This is likely a positive contributor to the overall mental health of priests. Moreover, of those priests who said they suffered from childhood trauma or dysfunction, a large number (72%) reported that they had been in counseling. This, too, is a positive sign for the priesthood in particular and the Church in general.

While priests' mental health appears largely stable and slightly better than that of the general population, they were not immune to deleterious psychological effects of the pandemic. Nevertheless, as a group, priests appeared to be less psychologically distressed by the pandemic than their counterparts. It appears that mental health resilience in a crisis is greater among priests than in the general population. This study investigated some of the possible reasons for priestly resilience in a crisis.

TWO CRISES AND THEIR EFFECTS ON PRIESTS

This study sought to research some of the effects of the sexual abuse crisis and the pandemic on priests. Thirty-one percent of the priest-respondents strongly agreed or agreed that they were being negatively affected by the pandemic at the time of the survey, compared with 19% of the sample who said they were negatively affected by the abuse crisis. So a significant number of priests are suffering emotionally in the wake of these two crises. However, by the time of this survey, the pandemic appeared to be eclipsing the abuse crisis in the minds of the priests. The strong majority of priests felt they were receiving sufficient assistance during the pandemic, although 14% did not.

The respondents were given a test to measure the presence of secondary trauma—the ProQOL 5. Were priests suffering the negative effects of secondary trauma as a result of ministering to others during these crises? The answer is no. As a group, they scored in the low range of secondary trauma. However, about 29% scored in the moderate range. So some of the priests experienced moderate distress as a result of ministering during these crises. However, it appears that the large majority of priests will not suffer long-term traumatic symptoms. Despite the very real stress and pain of these crises, most priests are resilient and able to weather these events.

This is not to say that these crises have not affected priests. The sexual abuse crisis has had a deleterious effect on many priests' views, especially of Church leadership and the priesthood. A majority of priests (55%) affirm that the sexual abuse scandal has negatively impacted their view of Church leadership. A lesser 29% affirm that it has had a negative effect on their view of priesthood, and a few (8%) say it has negatively influenced their faith.

A closer look at the variables affecting views of the abuse crisis indicated that priests who had a good relationship with their own bishop were less likely to have a more negative view of bishops in general as a result of the crisis. Priests' relationships with their own bishops remained relatively strong over the course of the three surveys (2004, 2009, 2021), averaging about three quarters of priests affirming a good relationship with their bishop. Given the critical and sacred nature of the bond between a bishop and his priests, it behooves individual bishops to prioritize spending time and fostering solid connections with their priests.

It was noted previously that depression rates doubled for priests during the pandemic. Looking at the individual items in the BSI-18 Depression scale, the most elevated item was "feeling lonely." During the pandemic, loneliness was one of the greatest trials for priests. Many priests felt isolated from their people. While a priest is meant to be a source of spiritual support for the people, the reverse is also true: the people are a great source of support for the priests. During the pandemic, this critical source of support was often restricted.

Loneliness is a critical factor for the psychological health of priests. It ought to be a strong consideration for any seeking to promote the welfare of priests.

RELATIONAL LIVES OF PRIESTS

The data in this study continued to affirm the importance of solid interpersonal relationships for the health and happiness of priests, and the deleterious effects of loneliness. Priests who reported good relationships with other priests and the laity were statistically more likely to say they were happy and that their morale was good. Also, their scores on the BSI-18 were better, thus indicating higher levels of mental health.

Priests with good interpersonal relationships were also more likely to say that they found their ministries to be satisfying. As a shepherd of souls, the priest has a "people" job. Being able to make solid connections with people is a critical aspect of a successful ministry.

The comments written on the surveys consistently showed that priests suffered from a lack of connection with the laity due to mandated COVID-19 precautions. As one priest wrote, "We need humanity back." Nevertheless, when looking at the self-report of their human relationships in the midst of the pandemic, we see that priests continued to report high levels of interpersonal connections and low levels of loneliness. For example, in the 2021 survey, 96% strongly agreed or agreed with the statement, "I have good lay friends who are an emotional support for me personally," and 91% strongly agreed or agreed with the statement, "I have close priest friends." This is actually an increase from the 2009 survey. In 2009, 93% said they had good lay friends, and 88% said they had close priest friends. So priests are self-reporting slightly higher levels of connections with friends. I suspect that priests answered this question based upon their overall experience beyond the pandemic. They realized that the interpersonal isolation of the pandemic was temporary. Such temporary pauses in connection do not obviate one's good relationships and may actually help people to value them more.

The two previous surveys highlighted the harmful effects of loneliness. When asked directly in the 2021 survey, 21% of priests professed to suffer from loneliness. They strongly agreed or agreed with the statement, "I suffer from loneliness." In response to the BSI-18 item about loneliness, 5% said they experienced feeling lonely "quite a bit" or "extremely." So, depending on how the question is framed, 5–21% of priests experience loneliness as a problem. While this is a minority of priests, it is not an insignificant issue for the presbyterate.

However, when compared with the laity, priests fare very well. In 2018 Cigna reported on an epidemic of loneliness among the laity in the United States, with 54% of respondents reporting that they are lonely. In January of 2020, Cigna found that the numbers actually got worse, with 61% reporting feeling lonely. Rates were higher among men than women.[2] One of the sustaining joys of priesthood is the priest's connection with the people. He is a source of spiritual support for them; they are a needed source of human sustenance for the priest.

SPIRITUAL LIVES OF PRIESTS

The spiritual practices of priests in the United States, as a group, are strong. By inference, their spiritual lives appear to be very healthy. For example, 95% strongly agree or agree that the Eucharist is the center of their lives; 95% strongly agree or agree to having a good relationship with God; and 82% strongly agree or agree that "celibacy has been a grace for me personally." Given the surrounding culture in the United States, this is quite remarkable, and it suggests that the majority of priests embrace the practice and spirituality of priestly celibacy.

Moreover, priests' self-reported spiritual practices consistently increased from the 2009 survey to the 2021 survey. For example, more priests are praying the Liturgy of the Hours, from 58% in 2009 to 68% in 2021. More priests are praying privately at least thirty minutes a day, from 51% in 2009 to 61% in 2021. And more priests profess to having a positive experience of celibacy, from 75% in 2009 to 82% in 2021. However, this does not mean that some priests do not struggle with their celibate calling. As one priest wrote on his survey, "Yes, celibacy is a struggle."

It has been reported elsewhere that younger priests today have a more traditional theological outlook. This 2021 study confirmed that young priests were more likely to engage in traditional spiritual practices. For example, comparing priests ordained 40–50 years with priests ordained 1–10 years, 97% of the younger priests make an annual retreat versus 86% of the older priests. Also, 70% of the younger priests have a regular spiritual director versus 59% of the older priests. Strikingly, 71% of younger priests receive the Sacrament of Penance monthly versus 23% of older priests. And 79% of younger priests pray the Liturgy of the Hours versus 59% of older priests. So younger priests were consistently more likely to follow some of the traditional spiritual practices of the clergy. No doubt, the influx of these younger, more traditional priests is driving up the percentages of priests engaged in these practices.

Graphing the trend in priestly cohorts engaged in more traditional spiritual practices indicates that a shift happened around 1990. As someone who worked with seminary communities during those years, I can concur that the 1990s did witness a shift toward a more traditional priestly spirituality.

Equally important is what is not significantly different between the younger and older priests. The two cohorts were statistically equivalent in their self-reported levels of happiness, relationship with God, and devotion to the Eucharist. While these two groups were sometimes different in their theological stance and spiritual practices, these core values—relationship with God, happiness, and Eucharistic devotion—remained strong for all the priests. They remain a strength for priesthood spanning many decades.

PREDICTING VULNERABILITY IN A CRISIS

There were six individual items in the 2021 survey that directly assessed how the two crises were affecting the priests:

- "The abuse crisis has negatively impacted my view of the priesthood."

- "The abuse crisis has negatively impacted my view of Church leadership."

- "The abuse crisis has negatively impacted my faith."

- "The COVID-19 pandemic has been traumatic for me personally."

- "The abuse crisis has negatively affected my emotional well-being."

- "I feel overwhelmed by the COVID-19 pandemic and need more support."

After statistical analysis including a factor analysis, Pearson's r correlations, and a Cronbach's alpha, the data showed that these six questions could be combined into one larger variable that I named Traumatized by the Crises. Those who reported being traumatized by one crisis, that is, the abuse crisis or the pandemic, were more likely to be traumatized by the other. This suggests that there are some priests, and likely human beings in general, who are more susceptible to suffering a personal trauma in the midst of a crisis, regardless of what kind of crisis it is.

Running correlations with this new combined variable, Traumatized by the Crises, led to identifying some of the variables that may contribute to increased vulnerability in a crisis. Some of the strongest predictors of this vulnerability were levels of personal connections. Priests who experienced stronger bonds within their priestly fraternity and who were less lonely were less vulnerable to being traumatized in the midst of a crisis. Going into a crisis being personally isolated from others results in a greater personal vulnerability to suffering trauma.

Inspecting the data reveals signs that priestly fraternity in this country needs to be strengthened. Only 69% of priests strongly agreed or agreed that "priests in my diocese/religious order are supportive of each other." The divisions in priesthood sometimes mirror the social divisions in the wider society, including the split between "red" and "blue," "conservative" and "liberal." Going from diocese to diocese in the past few decades, I have noticed that a constant theme in priest gatherings is a desire for stronger priestly unity and mutual support. Presbyterates ought to make enhancing priestly fraternity and unity a priority, recognizing that unity does not mean everyone has to think alike.

The presence of unhealed inner wounds also surfaced as a factor in increasing one's vulnerability in a crisis. More specifically, those with low self-esteem, a lack of inner peace, internal sexual conflicts, or a history of childhood trauma were more likely to suffer trauma in the midst of a crisis. Several priests witnessed to how important undergoing psychotherapy was for their wellness and happiness. Fortunately, 39% of priests said they had been in psychotherapy during their priesthood. This indicates that psychotherapeutic services appear to be available to a large number of priests, thus promoting the mental health of the priesthood as a whole.

Finally, the data suggested that a strong spiritual life contributed to crisis resilience. This includes a strong relationship with God, a daily regimen of private prayer, a positive embracing of celibacy, praying the Liturgy of the Hours and going frequently to Confession, and a devotion to the Blessed Virgin Mary and the Eucharist—that is, traditional spiritual practices of priesthood.

The data allowed comparison of younger priests with older priests in terms of having been traumatized by the two crises. There was no statistical difference between their cohorts. They were equally affected or not by these crises.

WHY ARE PRIESTS CRISIS RESILIENT?

Both the child sexual abuse crisis and the pandemic have been unprecedented in the lives of American Catholics in general and for priests in particular. Such unheard-of traumatic events in our time should not be underestimated. Despite these extraordinary stressors, there was no Great Resignation of priests. Morale and happiness levels among priests did not appreciably suffer. And their levels of mental health remained relatively strong. One important task of this study is to explain why. What made them crisis resilient?

It is of particular interest, as noted in the previous section, that in reference to the abuse crisis and the pandemic, priests who reported being negatively affected by one of the two crises were more likely to be negatively affected by the other. This suggested that there are variables that predict the vulnerability of a priest in any crisis. We delineate and discuss these variables in detail.

To explore why priests have been so resilient in the midst of trauma, we look again at each of the variables predicting vulnerability and, conversely, resilience. We then set forth the degree of incorporation and integration of these potential strengths. For example, if personal connections are critical for resilience, how strong were these connections for the priests during these crises? Or if one's relationship with God is a key to resilience, how strong were these relationships for the priests in the survey? The data in the 2021 survey showed the priests' great strength in these important areas and thus many reasons for their crisis resilience.

Here are some data from the 2021 survey demonstrating priests' great strengths and thus why priests as a group are crisis resilient:

- Loneliness rates are relatively low. Of those surveyed, 21% strongly agreed or agreed with the statement, "I suffer from loneliness," which is much lower than reported loneliness rates of the general population.

- Self-esteem of priests is high. Of the priest-respondents, 89% strongly agreed or agreed with the item "I feel a sense of inner peace," and 86% strongly agreed or agreed with "I have a good self-image."

- Priests' relationships with their individual bishops remain relatively strong. The data showed that 73% strongly agreed or agreed with the statement, "I have a good relationship with my bishop," and 80% strongly agreed or agreed with the statement, "I support my bishop's leadership."

- Priests' satisfaction with their ministries is extraordinarily high. Of those who responded to the survey, 92% very often or often "like my work as a [priest]"; 88% very often or often feel satisfied with their work; and 93% are happy to have chosen to be a priest.

- Childhood trauma rates among priests are not insignificant but are relatively low. Of the sample, only 19% strongly agreed or agreed with the statement, "I grew up in a dysfunctional family," whereas 94% reported having a good relationship with their mothers and 80% had a good relationship with their fathers.

- The spiritual practices and lives of priests were strong. For example, 95% affirm that "the Eucharist is the center of my life"; 90% have a devotion to the Blessed Virgin Mary; 82% believe that celibacy has been a grace for them personally; and

61% pray privately more than thirty minutes a day. The vast majority, 95%, report having a good relationship with God.

In addition, the research study of Nancy L. Sin and her colleagues during the pandemic found that providing COVID-19-related support to others predicted lower same-day negative affect.[3] Thus, those who were engaged in helping others during the pandemic were more likely to report feeling happy and satisfied. This alone is not a small factor in explaining why priests during these crises were reporting higher levels of happiness and satisfaction than the general population.

These and other findings in the survey show that the large majority of priests have solid interpersonal, ministerial, and spiritual strengths that are a bedrock during a time of crisis. These strengths help to explain why priests as a group are crisis resilient.

A New Mega Variable: Priest Wellness

The 2021 survey indicated that the following variables most strongly predicted whether the two crises affected the priests:

- Loneliness ($r = .44$)
- Self-Esteem ($r = -.42$)
- Relationship with Bishop ($r = -.33$)
- ProQOL Compassion Satisfaction ($r = -.33$)
- Childhood Trauma ($r = .28$)
- Traditional Spirituality ($r = -.27$)
- Priestly Fraternity ($r = -.24$)
- Sexual Conflicts ($r = .23$)
- Relationship with God ($r = -.23$)

These are essentially the same variables that most strongly predicted whether a priest is happy, whether he will be depressed or burned out, and the overall state of his mental health. Thus, these variables are most important for their impact on the life of a priest, both spiritually and psychologically.

In interpreting these results, we note that these variables are all intertwined in a mutual interaction. Happy priests are less likely to suffer from depression or anxiety, less likely to be burned out, and less likely to be traumatized in a crisis. Conversely, priests who suffer from depression or anxiety are more likely to be burned out, vulnerable to being traumatized in a crisis, and less likely to be happy in their lives and ministries. Traumatized priests are less likely to be happy and more likely to suffer from depression or anxiety and to be burned out. Burned-out priests are more likely to suffer from anxiety or depression, be unhappy in priesthood, and are more vulnerable to being traumatized in a crisis. All of these variables mutually interact and affect one another in the life of a priest.

Calculating the Pearson's r correlation for the four variables Priestly Happiness, Burnout, Mental Health, and Traumatized by the Crises indicates that these four major constructs are indeed highly correlated. The correlations for all of the pairs ranged from .46 to .65. After doing a factor analysis and then a Cronbach's alpha (.71), we see that these variables lend themselves to being combined into one overarching mega variable. This new variable might be named "Priestly Wellness, Happiness, and Resilience," or perhaps simply "Priestly Wellness." The new combined variable measures the overall psychological and spiritual health of a person, and in this case, a priest.

Calculating correlations and conducting a regression analysis on this new overarching variable yielded strong results.

Regressing all of the variables on Priestly Wellness yielded a high $r^2 = .64$ ($p < .001$). So we can predict 64% of what makes a priest psychologically and spiritually well! This is a very strong finding.

It was exciting to witness the statistical emergence of this mega concept. Frankly, it makes sense. A person is not split into subcategories. We look at different aspects of a person to help understand the whole individual better. But each of us is one unified person. We are body, psyche, and spirit all combined into one. Each aspect interpenetrates and informs the others. The emergence of this one mega variable is a statistical demonstration of this truth. Moreover, it can help focus more sharply the goals of a program of formation and ongoing growth for a priest—and likely for anyone.

When helping priests understand important personal strengths and weaknesses, we might look at these interconnected variables and ask how they fare in these areas. Are their houses "built on rock," or are they "built on sand" (Mt 7:24–27)? When a crisis comes along, does the wind destroy the house, or is it able to weather the storm? The resilience of most of our priests became apparent upon review of how they are currently doing with these variables. Their houses are built solidly upon rock.

2

THE SAMPLE
AND METHOD OF
THE 2021 SURVEY

The data for the study that informs this book were collected primarily from December 2020 through February 2021 during the COVID-19 pandemic and shortly after yet another abuse scandal erupted, this one in 2018. To accomplish this survey, a note to all US dioceses was sent out announcing that a priestly wellness study was being conducted. Dioceses were instructed to contact this researcher if interested and willing. A total of twenty-five dioceses eventually responded to this researcher and followed through to completion.

Taking part in the survey were large, medium-sized, and small dioceses located all over the United States: the West Coast, East Coast, Northeast, South, central part of the country, and north-central. Virtually every region of the United States was represented. Dioceses typically mailed out surveys to all of their priests, who were given an envelope to mail the completed form directly back to me. The survey responses were completely anonymous and confidential. Most dioceses sent out one to three reminders to all their priests to fill out the survey. However, there was no way to determine who did or did not fill it out; the respondents remained anonymous. The mean response rate of all the dioceses was a solid 57%.

The total number of usable responses in 2021 was 1,962, which is a large survey. At times in this study, I was able to compare the results of the 2021 survey with my 2009 study of 23 dioceses and 2,482 priests (the mean response rate in 2009 was an identical 57%). The results of the 2009 survey were published in *Why Priests Are Happy: A Study of the Psychological and Spiritual Health of Priests* (Ave Maria Press) in 2011. Also, there will be some comparable data from my 2004 study of 16 dioceses and 1,242 priests (the mean response rate in 2004 was 65%). Thus, this study provides some longitudinal research and trends in priesthood over the past almost two decades.

Regarding the 2021 sample, the mean age was sixty years old and the mean years ordained was twenty-nine years.[1] See table 2.1. There were 1,662 diocesan priests and 277 religious priests with 23 not answering to the question. The religious were on the diocesan priestly mailings presumably because they were ministering within the local diocese. Regarding nationality, 73% were born in the United States, 7% were born in a Hispanic nation, 5% came from an African nation, 5% were from India, and 2% were from Southeast Asia. Smaller percentages came from a variety of nations around the world such as Ireland, Italy, the Philippines, Germany, and Poland. Sixty respondents did not answer this question.

The survey encompasses a large cross-section of age, ethnicity, and region. Thus, this 2021 survey should be generally representative of the Catholic priests in the United States. As with any research, the strength of its findings is confirmed when other studies find similar results. I will endeavor to cite such confirmatory studies when available. I encourage future researchers to compare their findings to these three studies and to push forward in this important area of research.

Table 2.1. The 2021 sample by ordination decade

Years Ordained by Decades		Frequency	Percent	Valid Percent	Cumulative Percent
Valid	1-10	368	18.8	19.4	19.4
	11-20	372	19.0	19.7	39.1
	21-30	298	15.2	15.7	54.8
	31-40	306	15.6	16.2	71.0
	41-50	300	15.3	15.8	86.8
	51+	249	12.7	13.2	100.0
	Total	1893	96.5	100.0	
Missing		69	3.5		
System Total		1962	100.0		

THE STATISTICAL METHOD

The software package used to run the statistical routines was PASW 27 (Predictive Analytics SoftWare, SPSS). Whenever items in the survey were combined to form larger variables, a factor analysis was performed using a principal components analysis with two extraction methods: maximum likelihood and principal axis, typically with a varimax rotation. Then, a Cronbach's alpha was computed.

The combined larger variables are listed in appendix 2. If these are compared with the composite variables in the 2009 survey published in appendix 3 of my book *Why Priests Are Happy*, one will notice that many of the items used and subsequent composite variables are the same. This is a confirmation of the validity of combining these items. It also gives an opportunity to compare the findings in the 2009 survey with this 2021 survey.

Pearson's r correlations were often computed on continuous variables to determine if the variables were related. Two-tailed correlations were conducted, and all correlations reported were statistically significant at least at the level of $p < .05$ if not greater. A careful reader will note that many of the statistical findings and correlations reported in 2009 also held up in this 2021 study. Again, this supports the validity of the findings in both studies.

If variables were not continuous, such as yes/no answers or country of birth, then an ANOVA or T test was computed. If an ANOVA was found to be significant, then a post-hoc test was computed to determine where the significant differences were found.

Especially toward the end of the study, several multiple regression equations were performed. I used these to determine how a number of variables could predict such important constructs as priestly happiness, mental health, burnout, resilience in a crisis, and overall priestly wellness. It was affirming to see the extent to which the items in the survey could predict these important constructs. This research tells us quite a bit about what makes a happy and well priest.

It is worth emphasizing that a statistically significant correlation does not indicate a cause-and-effect relationship. In social science research, some caution in interpreting the findings of the data is always appropriate. While two variables may co-vary, it is possible that there is a third unidentified variable that is causing the correlation. Thus, it is important to inspect these correlations and to use one's theoretical understandings and previous research findings to interpret the data. This is essential in social science research because the more pristine laboratory conditions of "hard" scientific research are often not available in our field.

It is clear that many of the variables influence each other in complex and interdependent ways; that is, they exhibit multi-collinearity. In the final analysis, it is likely that these variables mutually influence one another. For example, a happy priest is less likely to burn out. And a burned-out priest is less likely to be happy. Which comes first? It is probable that the variables influence each other and are mutually reinforcing.

I have endeavored to be as transparent as possible with interpretation of the data. Others are welcome to draw their own conclusions. I know that some may question my conclusions, which they are welcome to do. Survey research has the limitation of not revealing why a respondent answered the question in one way or another. For example, when a priest says he is "happy," what does that mean? It may mean different things to different respondents. But what helps this research is the large number of respondents (1,962), which tends to wash out the outliers and nullify extremes in thinking.

The respondents were invited to write in their thoughts at the end of the survey, using their own words. These comments were invaluable in getting a sense of their minds and hearts. I have woven these comments throughout the book, allowing the priests to speak in their own voices. Between the statistics and the comments, I hope that readers takes away a deeper insight into the US priests of today, and perhaps even, by extension, a deeper insight into themselves. I know I did.

3

PRIESTHOOD AND HAPPINESS

PRIESTHOOD HAPPINESS LEVELS REMAIN HIGH

All three surveys (2004, 2009, and 2021) contained the item "Overall, I am happy as a priest." This gives us the ability to look at trends over several years in self-reported priestly happiness. Table 3.1 displays the results. There are several insights that might strike the reader when comparing these self-reported happiness levels. First, happiness levels among priests remain extraordinarily high. The percentage of priests who strongly agree or agree that they are happy steadily stays above 90%, despite the abuse crisis and the pandemic.

*Sometimes the reported figures will be slightly different in different places due to rounding effects. When decimals were .1-.4, the numbers were rounded down. When the decimals were .5-.9 the numbers were rounded up.

Table 3.1. Results of 2004, 2009, and 2021 surveys: "Overall, I am happy as a priest"

	Strongly agree (%)	Agree (%)	Unsure (%)	Disagree (%)	Strongly disagree (%)
2004 survey	39.2	50.8	5.2	4.5	.3
2009 survey	42.5	49.9	5.0	2.1	.5
2021 survey	55.7	38.1	3.3	2.1	.9

Source for 2004 and 2009 survey results: Stephen J. Rossetti, Why Priests are Happy: A Study of the Psychological and Spiritual Health of Priests. (Notre Dame, IN: Ave Maria Press, 2011), Table 6.1, p. 86.

If the reader is skeptical of these findings, I encourage a look at other surveys on priestly happiness over the past few decades. The results are similar, regardless of who conducts the survey. For example, in 2003, the *Hartford Courant* conducted an informal survey of 107 priests and found that "94 strongly agreed with the statement 'Most of the time, I am happy with my life as a priest.'"[1] Similarly, a CARA study of 960 priests published in 2012 found that 61% of priests said they were "very happy" and 36% said they were "pretty happy" in response to the question, "How happy are you with your life as a priest?" Less than 4% said they were "not too happy" or "not at all happy."[2] The CARA study concluded: "Priests are generally very happy with their lives and ministry. There is no overarching morale problem in the priesthood."[3]

The overall happiness of our priests has been resilient to the crises affecting the Church. This does not mean that priests are not suffering because of these crises. Rather, I believe that, when given the statement, "Overall, I am happy as a priest," most priests do not look at passing phenomena or transient emotional states. Rather, they are likely reflecting on their deeper, long-term experience. Fundamentally, at root, is the priest at peace with his priesthood? Did he make the right choice to enter the priesthood? The answer for more than 90% was, and remains, yes.

Supporting that statement are the respondents' answers to the statement, "I am thinking of leaving the priesthood." Only 3% strongly agreed or agreed. When given the statement, "If I had to do it all over again, I would still become a priest," again only 3% strongly disagreed or disagreed. The 2012 CARA study similarly found that 3% of the priests were "uncertain about my future" and no priests said, "I probably will leave."[4] There has not been a perceptible exodus of priests as a result of these two crises. This is remarkable. How would a secular business fare under similar circumstances of crisis and stress? The priest's connection to priesthood is often perceived as a stronger bond and likely a deeper spiritual reality compared with the holder of a secular job.

HAPPINESS OF AMERICANS DIVES DURING PANDEMIC

How do the happiness levels of priests compare with those of their lay counterparts? Lay happiness apparently took a sharp nosedive during the pandemic. The 2021 General Social Survey found that Americans who self-identified as "very happy" dropped sharply from 31% in 2018 to 19% in 2021, in the midst of the pandemic. Those who self-identified as "not too happy" rose from 13% to 24%.[5]

This discontent among the general population of Americans during the pandemic was likely one of the reasons for the Great Resignation of 2021. In an article for *America* magazine, John W. Miller noted that 4.7 million Americans quit their jobs that year, according to the Bureau of Labor Statistics. One of the reasons cited was "a massive burnout caused by the stress and anxiety of the global pandemic."[6] Some reports suggest that Protestant clergy shared in these feelings of burnout. In December of 2020, the *Washington Post* reported that there was an "exodus of clergy who left ministry in the past couple of years because of a powerful combination of pandemic demands and political stress . . . pastoral burnout has been high." The article quoted a Barna survey of Protestant pastors in which 38% said they had considered quitting full-time ministry in the past year.[7]

The prepandemic level of happiness among the general population was measured in 2018 by the General Social Survey. The survey found that 31% of respondents were "very happy," 56%

were "pretty happy," and 13% were "not too happy." Priests' self-reported happiness levels were higher. As indicated in table 3.1, when responding to a statement on overall happiness in our prepandemic survey of 2009, 42.5% of priests strongly agreed and 49.9% agreed, whereas 2.1% disagreed and .5% strongly disagreed.

The data show that priestly happiness levels are higher than those of the general population. Their happiness levels did not plummet during the pandemic, as they did among the general population. Catholic priests did not take part in the Great Resignation. Rather, as one pastor shared with me, priests knew they needed to help their flocks during this time of crisis. So they courageously did what they could, often very creatively, to minister to suffering people in a time of great stress.

It might remind us of the courageous and selfless efforts of first responders, such as doctors, nurses, and many others, who stepped up during the pandemic. Often they put their own needs aside to help others. Typically, after such a crisis is over, some first responders will manifest symptoms of delayed stress. This is something to watch for in the days ahead in our priests, as with all first responders.

But can we really trust these numbers of a high priestly happiness? Have priestly happiness levels remained as high, and as sustained during the crises, as they appear to have been? A continuing investigation of the numbers will give us some initial answers.

Priests Very Satisfied with Ministry

One place to start probing more deeply into priestly happiness is to look at their satisfaction or dissatisfaction with their daily duties. How do they like or dislike their daily ministry? Is it personally fulfilling?

Survey respondents were given the Professional Quality of Life Scale no. 5 (ProQOL 5). The ProQOL 5 is a widely used test developed by Dr. Beth Hudnall Stamm that measures positive and negative effects of helping others who are suffering or undergoing trauma. It has three subscales: Compassion Satisfaction, Burnout, and Secondary Traumatic Stress.[8]

The Compassion Satisfaction scale is "about the pleasure you derive from being able to do your work well. For example, you may feel like it is a pleasure to help others through your work."[9] The mean ProQOL 5 Compassion Satisfaction raw score for the entire sample of 1,962 priests in our 2021 survey was 42. See table 6.2. A raw score of 42 or above is in the top 25%. Therefore, compared to their lay peers, priests in the United States as a group are in the top quarter of people in satisfaction with their work/ministry. This is a positive finding.

It is not surprising that the Compassion Satisfaction scale is very highly correlated with priestly happiness ($r = .61$, $p < .01$). Priests who found much satisfaction in their particular ministries were highly likely to report being happy as priests. Looking at some of the items in the scale and how the priests responded should give us an important insight into the state of priestly satisfaction today. See table 3.2. It is abundantly clear that a major source of what makes priests happy is satisfaction with their ministries. A strong 88% to 93% of priests often or very often experience satisfaction in their ministries. Priests like their work; they feel they are making a difference; and they confirm that they are happy to have chosen to be a priest.

Table 3.2. Results of 2021 survey: The ProQOL 5 Compassion Satisfaction scale

	Never (%)	Rarely (%)	Sometimes (%)	Often (%)	Very often (%)
I like my work as a [priest].	.8	.8	6.7	35.3	56.4
My work makes me feel satisfied.	.5	1.5	9.9	39.4	48.7
I believe I can make a difference through my work.	.7	1.3	10.1	41.5	46.5
I am happy that I chose to do this work.	.4	1.1	6.0	26.0	66.5

Survey respondents were given the opportunity at the end of the survey to write comments, which were transcribed verbatim. A number of written comments echoed these positive sentiments:

- "I love what I do as a priest. I love my parishioners; they love me in return; this sustains me."

- "I've had wonderful years of ministry with people."

- "I am pleased to walk as a helper, brother, and friend to kids, teenagers, and adults."

- "I enjoy being a presider of the Eucharist and sacraments. The people are freely coming to encounter Christ."

- "I am very glad to be a preacher of the Gospel message and to proclaim the Good News."

- "I feel an essential part of society helping in the salvation of souls and feeding the People of God with the sacraments. This is very rewarding. I think this is now more necessary than ever."

- "I find the most joy in the typical priestly activities: Mass, sacraments, Communion calls, sick visits, dinner with families, high school ministry, and youth group."

- "I often receive Christmas cards from families I served 36 years ago. It has been a good life."

Virtually no priests wrote that they did not like ministry with the people. While a few wanted a different assignment, and more than a few struggled to keep up with the sometimes overwhelming demands of their roles, they universally found their connection with the People of God to be overall a positive and nourishing experience.

How does this compare with the laity and secular jobs? Distilling the findings of several job satisfaction surveys, including PayScale, CareerBliss, and *US News & World Report*, one article reported that 65% of Americans were satisfied with their jobs.[10] A modest 20% were passionate about their work. It is important to note that among the positions that had the highest levels of happiness, the highest was "clergy" at 74%.[11] When trying to explain these results, some social psychologists posit that jobs dedicated to helping other people provide higher levels of happiness.[12]

PRIESTLY HAPPINESS IS RISING

Table 3.1 indicates a significant trend that ought to be explored. From 2004 to 2009 to 2021, the "strongly agree" column of priestly happiness has increased markedly. While the overall percentage of priests who are happy (strongly agree plus agree) remains solidly above 90%, priest-respondents actually reported a growing and stronger sense of happiness over the past seventeen years. The "strongly agree" group went from 39.2% (2004) to 42.5% (2009) to 55.7% (2021). This is a significant movement upward.

In a time of crisis, this is counterintuitive. One might presume that the abuse crisis of the past two decades and the COVID-19 pandemic, which was declared in early March of 2020, would dampen happiness and thwart any upward movement. However, the opposite appears to be true. It is remarkable that in a time when one might argue that overall morale in the United States is declining or at least struggling, that priestly morale, as reported by the priests themselves, is actually rising. How can we account for this?

The question of why priestly happiness is rising is an important one. The common assumption that priests are unhappy is entirely reasonable, given the increasing secularization of society, the declining numbers of priests and their heavier workloads, and the ongoing crises of sexual abuse and the pandemic. But if priestly happiness is truly rising, then we might look more closely at what contributes directly to personal happiness. It might not be what is publicly touted as essential to morale. And it might give us an insight into what actually contributes to personal happiness in anyone's life.

In the 2009 study, I reported that younger priests were helping to increase happiness levels. The younger cohorts were reporting higher levels of happiness than the middle-aged priests.[13] However, in this 2021 study, there were no large differences in happiness levels among age cohorts. Each age cohort reported very high levels of satisfaction that were statistically similar. I was surprised and checked the numbers several times, running a variety of statistical routines to make sure this was correct. It is.

The 2012 CARA study also concluded that happiness levels were rising among priests. The study concluded that one reason for rising priestly morale was the increasing adherence to a more "traditional theology" among younger priests, who report higher satisfaction levels.[14] Nevertheless, there was no significant difference in happiness levels among age cohorts in this study. The self-reported happiness levels of the older priests were slightly higher than those of priests in the first ten years of ordination, but the difference was not statistically significant.

So what happened to the less happy older priests from the 2009 study? In this current study, they are *all* reporting higher levels of satisfaction. For example, of the priests ordained 21–30 years in the 2009 study, 35.8% self-reported as very happy. Among this same cohort a decade later, 51.6% reported as being very happy. This is slightly less than the overall rate of 55.7% in 2021, but the percentage is still markedly up from 35.8% in 2009.

The 2012 CARA study offered data showing rising morale as a priest ages. The study authors concluded, "Priests tend to become more satisfied as they grow older."[15] Moreover, the data in this study affirm that there are unique challenges for the newly ordained that can have deleterious effects on priestly well-being. This will be reported in some depth later in this book. The 2018 CARA study of the recently ordained affirmed that some young priests are struggling. The authors found that "four in five responding newly ordained priests report being satisfied with their life as priest (59% 'very satisfied' and 22% 'somewhat satisfied')."[16] Thus, 19% were somewhat dissatisfied or very dissatisfied. So, while younger, more traditional priests tend to have higher morale, the challenges of being newly ordained can dampen overall satisfaction rates for this cohort.

Another reason for the increase in morale might be the rising average age of US priests. Since the average age of priests in the United States has increased in the past few decades, and since priests tend to become happier with age according to CARA, this could be another factor contributing to the rising morale.[17]

One step in attempting to substantiate the findings of a rising priestly morale was looking at the responses for priestly happiness in the 2021 survey against a similar item in both the 2004 and 2009 surveys: "My morale as a priest is good." See table 3.3. Once again, there is a similar rising morale among priests in the seventeen years of these three surveys. This extends the findings of Dean Hoge of Catholic University.

Table 3.3. Results of 2004, 2009, and 2021 surveys: "My morale as a priest is good"

	Strongly agree (%)	Agree (%)	Unsure (%)	Disagree (%)	Strongly disagree (%)
2004 survey*	19.3	60.7	8.2	9.8	1.9
2009 survey	31.3	57.6	6.4	3.8	.9
2021 survey	42.1	45.5	6.0	4.7	1.7

*The question in the 2004 survey was slightly different: "My morale is good" vs. "My morale as a priest is good," the latter being found in the 2009 and 2021 surveys.

In the 2001 study he authored for the National Federation of Priests' Councils, he found rising levels of happiness in priests in the United States. In Dr. Hoge's study, the percentage of priests who said they were very happy went from 28% in 1970, to 39% in 1985 and 1993, and finally to 45% in 2001.[18] In my study, these numbers dipped in 2004 to 39%, then in 2009 went back up to 43%, and then to 56% in 2021. The abuse crisis of 2002 may indeed have had a temporary effect on depressing priestly happiness, but morale has since recovered and gone to new heights. This latest increase in morale/happiness appears to be felt by the entire presbyterate of all decades.

It is likely that the very painful sexual abuse crisis that began in Boston in 2002 and swept through the country had a significant effect on temporarily dampening priestly happiness. But morale has risen to new highs even in our current turbulent times. Certainly, the years after Vatican Council II were turbulent for priesthood. Many thought celibacy would become optional. There was more experimenting with the liturgy, seminary formation, and other aspects of Church life. Resignations among priests and religious became a regular experience, devastating some religious communities. Those years were painful and difficult. The numbers in these studies suggest that they represent a nadir in priestly happiness. Since then, it has been a steady march upward, with possible temporary setbacks as a result of public sex abuse scandals.

INTERNATIONAL PRIESTS ARE HAPPY

Are priests in the United States who were born in other countries more or less happy than native-born priests? I compared the response rates of "strongly agree" to the statement, "Overall, I am happy as a priest," for clergy born in different countries. There were 71 priest-respondents born in Africa, and 77% said they were very happy. There were 62 priest-respondents born in India, and 73% said they were very happy. There were 92 respondents born in a Hispanic nation, and 70% declared they were very happy. There were 27 respondents born in Southeast Asia, including Vietnam and Indonesia, and 63% said they were very happy. Finally, 52% of priests born in the United States said they were very happy. For priests born in other nations not mentioned, the sample sizes were too small to make meaningful statements.

So a larger percentage of priests born in Africa, India, Hispanic countries, and Southeast Asia report being very happy than US-born priests. This is a significant finding. Leaving family, country, and culture for a new land is not an easy transition, regardless of the local conditions. There are priests from other nations who come to the United States and then decide to return home. Fortunately, the ones who remain report very high levels of contentment. So it appears that their transition to this country and its presbyterate, for the most part, is successful. Assisting priests from other nations in their transition to this country, including giving them a warm welcome and inviting them into the presbyterate and its daily life, is important.

Some priest-respondents wrote positive comments about international priests in their diocese and priestly fraternity:

- "Our diocese has native priests and a large number of international priests, Indian and African. We associate well together."

- "There is a good relationship among the presbyterate. It's international and multicultural in nature."

"I LOVE BEING A PRIEST"

As noted, respondents were invited to write in comments at the end of the survey. There were 443 respondents who wrote usable comments.[19] Of these, 58% wrote a comment that was positive in tone, while 29% wrote critically about some aspect of their lives or the Church, and 13% were neither completely positive nor negative. Many of those who wrote critical comments nevertheless indicated they were happy as priests (since only 6% of priests did not indicate they were happy) but used the comments section to voice a particular criticism or unhappiness that they experienced.

The most common sentence written by a priest-respondent was, "I love being a priest." This phrasing was echoed across dioceses, among younger and older priests. Another common statement was, "I am very happy the Lord called me to the priesthood." These most-repeated statements help support the statistical findings of a large number of priests who "love" being a priest.

Moreover, these statements suggest that it is *being* a priest that promotes so much happiness. While there were many comments about satisfaction in *doing* what priests do, the most common statement was, "I love being a priest." Thus, while priests were almost universally positive about their ministries, their fundamental positive experience as a priest was more about who they *are* and are *called to be*.

4

UNHAPPY PRIESTS

Six Percent Not Happy

It is important to note that not all priests are happy. In response to the 2021 survey item "Overall, I am happy as a priest," 3.3% responded "unsure," 2.1% responded "disagree," and 0.9% responded, "strongly disagree." So there are about 6% of priest-respondents who do not report being happy as a priest.

As previously mentioned, 29% of the written comments were negative. Although many of the respondents professed to being happy overall as priests, their written comments focused on something that made them unhappy. For example, one priest wrote, "I've had wonderful years of ministry with people. One most negative experience for me is the bishop." So this priest had a wonderful priesthood but did not like his bishop.

While it was rare, there were a few priests who were downright bitter about their experience in the priesthood. Three percent of the respondents were clear that, if faced with the decision again to become a priest, the answer would be no. Some wrote about their unhappiness with celibacy; others spoke about feelings of isolation; others strongly criticized the Church hierarchy; still others were scandalized by the sexual abuse crisis. Their comments expressed frustration, anger, and bitterness.

One upset priest said the Church hierarchy had abandoned its priests in the wake of the abuse scandal and had "thrown so many of my brother priests under the bus." Another wrote, "I feel trapped in the Church and would like to retire but I am not old enough." Still another wrote, "Celibacy is nonsense."

A very strong 94% of the entire 2021 sample strongly agreed or agreed with the statement, "Overall I am happy as a priest." Who then are the other 6% who said they were unsure, disagreed, or strongly disagreed with that statement? Can we identify some variables that will predict if a priest will be unhappy?

LACK OF INNER PEACE

To begin to discover the variables that predict unhappiness, that is, what makes an unhappy priest, I correlated all the variables on the survey with the composite variable Priestly Happiness, which consists of a combination of two items: "Overall, I am happy as a priest" and "My morale as a priest is good." (See appendix 2 for the Cronbach's alpha of all the composite variables in this survey.)

Several significant findings emerged. One of the strongest findings was the importance of the internal dimension of happiness. "I feel a sense of inner peace" was the survey's strongest predictor of priestly happiness ($r = .61$, $p < .01$). This is almost identical to the findings in the 2009 study ($r = .59$) and confirms the truth of this finding.

A popular maxim is, "Happiness is an inside job." The findings of both of these surveys affirm it. One might say that happiness depends as much on what people bring to a situation as what they encounter when they arrive.

In a similar vein, the correlation between the variables "I have a good self-image" and Priestly Happiness was very strong ($r = .50$, $p < .001$). If we do not like what we see around us, it may be that a negative interior lens is clouding our vision. If we do not love ourselves, it is well-nigh impossible to love our neighbor, as the scriptures admonish us to do. If we are unhappy with the person we are and are not at peace inside, how can we find happiness around us?

This is a challenging finding. If we are unhappy, we might first look inside and see if there is anything internal dragging us down. Of course, the people, structures, and processes around us are far from perfect. But then again, we, too, are imperfect. The road to God's peace begins with realizing our own sinfulness and asking for forgiveness and healing. Nevertheless, it is common for people to focus outward in their unhappiness. After reading every one of the 443 written comments, I concluded that the unhappy respondents in this survey largely did so. They associated their unhappiness with factors outside of themselves.

This finding, the importance of good self-esteem and inner peace for ultimate happiness as a priest, highlights the need for effective screening and psychological formation of candidates for the priesthood. Those whose self-image is heavily damaged will not be good candidates. There are others who are good candidates but need remedial healing in this area. Fortunately, most seminaries today have mental health professionals to assist when needed. This study affirms the need for such psychological services.

ISOLATION

Another strong finding from this study is the connection between isolation and unhappiness. Many of the variables that most strongly predicted happiness had to do with relationships. The priest who develops solid relationships with others is more likely to be a happy priest. "I have close priest friends" ($r = .30, p < .001$)

and "I have good lay friends" ($r = .26$, $p < .001$) both correlated positively and significantly with Priestly Happiness.

Conversely, of the respondents who reported that they did not have close priest friends (strongly disagree or disagree), only 29% said they were very happy (strongly agree), compared to 55% for the total sample. Similarly, only 30% of those who reported not having good lay friends said they were very happy, compared to 55% for the total sample. Lack of good relationships cut the happiness rate almost in half! Disconnection with others and the resulting isolation are strong factors in predicting priestly dissatisfaction. Simply put, priests without close friends—either fellow priests or laypeople—are not likely to be happy priests.

The presence of loneliness is strongly connected to priestly unhappiness. Two items in the survey were combined to form the composite variable Loneliness: "I suffer from loneliness" and the BSI-18 item "feeling lonely." The variables Priestly Happiness and Loneliness were strongly correlated ($r = -.50$, $p < .001$).[1] The correlation was negative: as loneliness increases, priestly happiness decreases.

Of those respondents who indicated they strongly agreed or agreed with the statement "I suffer from loneliness," only 29% said they were very happy. This is compared with 55% for the entire sample. So being lonely also cuts the rate of happiness in half. (It should be noted that loneliness did not completely account for priestly unhappiness, and thus there are other factors to consider. We will investigate these in the course of this study.)

Loneliness was mentioned a few times among negative comments on the survey. Here is a sample:

- "I struggle with celibacy."

- "This is a difficult and lonely life. It has gotten a lot harder and even more lonely in the heat of the abuse crisis and COVID."

- "Today I am very lonely and would love a female companion."

In the wake of the abuse crisis and in the light of St. John Paul II's landmark 1992 apostolic exhortation, *Pastores Dabo Vobis*, human formation has been given greater attention. This document named human formation as the "necessary foundation" of priestly formation. While seminarians in the United States are currently being told about the importance of solid human relationships for a balanced priestly life, are they actually being trained how to cultivate such relationships?

Some seminarians come from isolated backgrounds; others have no siblings or peer relationships. Thus, some of them have little to no history or skills in making healthy human relationships. We cannot assume that candidates for the priesthood today have experience in fostering and nurturing friendships. If I could add one course to the seminary today, it would be a practical course in building relationships.

RELATIONSHIP WITH GOD

Priesthood is intrinsically connected to the spiritual life, necessarily encompassing one's direct relationship with God and the Catholic Church. It only makes sense therefore to hypothesize that priests who have a strong relationship with God, a solid spiritual life, and a positive connection with the Church (including its incarnation as an institutional body) would be happier. Conversely, those who do not have these strong spiritual connections would likely be less happy. Do the results of the survey confirm that hypothesis?

The answer is clearly yes. As for connection to God, the correlation of "I have a good relationship with God" and the variable Priestly Happiness was very strong ($r = .44$, $p < .001$). Similarly, the correlation of the item "I feel a sense of closeness to God" was also very strong ($r = .46$, $p < .001$.) A new composite variable named Relationship with God combined these two survey items. Statistical analysis and face value suggested that these two items could be combined (a factor analysis plus a Cronbach's alpha = .76). This combined variable was even more strongly correlated with Priestly Happiness ($r = .50$, $p < .001$). Priests who self-report not having a good relationship with God are much less likely to be happy. It is not surprising that a strong positive connection between a priest and God is essential to the happiness of the priest.

Priests who did not report having a good relationship with God were few; that is, 1% strongly disagreed or disagreed with the statement, "I have a good relationship to God," and the same percentage did not feel a sense of closeness to God. About 4% said they were "unsure" about both of these items. Only 45% of priests giving these responses reported being happy (strongly agreed or agreed), compared with 94% of the overall sample. So happiness levels of those without a good relationship with God were reduced by more than half! On his survey in the comments section, one priest wrote: "Priesthood should be a love affair with our Lord. Fall in love with our Lord. Stay in love with our Lord."

As for living a spiritual life, priests who prayed privately for thirty minutes or more each day reported a high degree of happiness: a strong 61% reported being very happy ("strongly agree"). This dipped markedly for those who were praying less. Of those who reported spending fifteen minutes or less in private prayer daily, only 37% reported being very happy ("strongly agree").

Thus, happiness rates dropped noticeably for those who engaged in a minimum of daily prayer. One priest-respondent wrote on his survey: "I work extensively with victims, with handling allegations. . . . Through it all, my prayer has kept me grounded. Despite the difficulties of today, I have great hope for tomorrow."

Moreover, the amount of daily private prayer engaged in by the priests was significantly correlated with their reported relationship with God ($r = .25$, $p < .001$). Those who prayed more reported a stronger connection to God. Nurturing one's relationship with God through prayer is obviously important and contributes significantly to one's happiness as a priest. And those priests who do not develop a prayer life or a relationship with God are much more likely to be unhappy. On his survey one priest wrote: "I think the key is my prayer life, my belief in the Real Presence of Christ in the Eucharist and in me and in others. . . . prayer, the Eucharist, a spiritual director, friends, and humor are essential in the life of a priest, I think."

RELATIONSHIP WITH THE BISHOP

One aspect of a connection with the Church is the priest's perceived connection with his bishop. The priests were given the statement, "I have a good relationship with my bishop." That variable's ability to predict happiness was surprisingly strong ($r = .46$, $p < .001$). This is reminiscent of a similar finding in the 2009 study in which the correlation was similar ($r = .33$), thus supporting this finding.[2]

It is also striking that 82% of the priests in the 2021 study who reported having a good relationship with their bishop ("strongly agree") also reported being very happy ("strongly agree"). Conversely, only 25% of the priests reported being very happy if they did not have a good relationship with their bishop. The happiness levels of priests plummet when they do not have a positive connection to their bishop.

In the written comments at the end of the survey form, the majority of those that were negative focused on priests' unhappiness with the Church hierarchy, especially with their own bishop and his chancery staff. The most common complaint from these priests was that their bishop does not listen to them or does not support and value them. Here are some examples of these comments:

- "The chancery doesn't care about us as people."
- "There was no support from my diocese for clergy during the pandemic."
- "There is a lack of spiritual fatherhood or healthy relationship with my bishop."
- "My bishop rarely communicates to his priests directly."
- "I have been disappointed by superiors; I have not always felt understood or supported."
- "The bishop does not support his priests."
- "My only source of tension is the diocese. I feel as if they do not care about the priests."

As we shall see later in this study, the strong majority of priests professed to having a good relationship with their bishop (73% strongly agree or agree). But when priests were unhappy, the comments section suggests that they often associated their unhappiness with the person of the bishop and his chancery.

The Father Wound

As a psychologist, I was interested in any possible connection between a priest's relationship with his biological father during his developmental years and his subsequent perception of his relationship with his bishop. Did the priest carry over any difficulties with male authority from childhood to adulthood? Did the "father wound" carry over into adulthood?

There was a statistically significant correlation ($r = .21$, $p < .001$) between the variable "Growing up, I had a good relationship with my father" and the variable "I have a good relationship with my bishop." A large percentage (79%) of priests who strongly agreed to having a good relationship with their fathers also strongly agreed or agreed to having a good relationship with their bishops. Yet 60% of those who strongly disagreed with having a good relationship with their fathers strongly agreed or agreed to having a good relationship with their bishops. So the percentage of priests who were happy with their bishop dropped almost 20% when they did not have a good relationship with their biological fathers.

From a clinical perspective, it is not surprising that those who did not have a good relationship with their father might have greater difficulty with their relationship with another father figure, that is, the bishop. While the difference between those who did and did not have a good paternal relationship should not be overstated since the correlation was only .21, the decline was statistically significant.

As a clinician, I have worked with many priests who struggled with authority issues stemming from dysfunctional childhood relationships. My experience suggests that the father wound is difficult to overcome, although not impossible. Some of those who have overcome such a wound were directly touched in prayer by

God the Father. Many had a powerful experience of the Father's personal love for them, which contributed greatly to their healing. Even with such a grace, some traces of authority issues may remain.

So far in this study, we have looked at some of the dynamics of unhappy priests. While they are few in percentage, they are, of course, important. Our concern and care for them, as people and as priests, should be direct and generous. Also, understanding what contributes to their unhappiness is helpful for the effective screening, formation, and ongoing formation of priests. Conversely, the variables that correlate highly with their unhappiness will likewise be significant predictors of what makes a happy priest, as we shall see later on in this work.

5

THE MENTAL HEALTH OF
PRIESTS TODAY

T he mental health of our priests remains a vital concern. The abuse crisis has highlighted the importance of good mental health and thus the need for psychological screening and human formation in the seminary. During the 2002 abuse crisis, a Texas newspaper erroneously reported that most seminaries and dioceses did not psychologically screen their candidates. In fact, most dioceses in the United States had already put in place professional psychological screening for anyone applying for the priesthood. This author himself, upon applying for admittance to priestly formation in 1979, went through a battery of psychological tests and a clinical interview with a psychologist.

THE ROLE OF PSYCHOLOGY IN OUR FAITH

Fostering the mental health of our priests is critical, but at times within the ranks of the Church, well-intentioned individuals will cast aspersions on any input of psychology, suggesting that it is contrary to the true faith. Improperly used, psychology can indeed be destructive of the faith. The field of psychology is not theology; it remains a secular science that, like all sciences, can contribute to our knowledge of the truth. Secular sciences can and should be used as adjunctive aids to our formation and to the overall health of the Church. We use psychology not as a substitute for our spirituality, but as an adjunct. If we ignore the secular sciences, especially the medical sciences and psychology, we do a great disservice to the People of God.

A MENTAL HEALTH INSTRUMENT IN THE 2021 SURVEY: THE BSI-18

As we look at the current mental health of our priests, it is worth repeating that this study was conducted during the COVID-19 pandemic. Most of the data were gathered in the December 2020–February 2021 time frame, while the pandemic was in full force. This allows us a unique insight into the effects of the pandemic on priestly wellness and mental health.

The priests in this 2021 study were given a standardized test called the Brief Symptom Inventory 18 (BSI-18). With 18 individual items, it was developed as a "highly sensitive screen for psychiatric disorders and psychological integration."[1] Leonard Derogatis, the test developer, noted, "Close to 80% of the psychiatric disorders that occur in community and medical populations are anxiety and depressive disorders with depression representing the most prevalent disorder in primary care."[2] The BSI-18 scales should be good overall indicators of mental health.

Our population of Catholic priests was compared to the BSI-18 community norm sample of 605 adult males. This is a nonclinical sample of males taken from the general community, similar to our sample of priests. The BSI-18 is particularly appropriate in our study precisely because it can be used in nonclinical samples and has norms for males. I have found that one of the great lacunae of past studies of priesthood is the lack of comparing the data with norms. How can one interpret data when there is nothing to compare it with? Using standardized norms is an important start.

The BSI-18 has four scales. The first scale is Somatization (SOM), which measures the presence of distress caused by bodily dysfunction. These dysfunctions are often present in somaticized versions of anxiety and depression and thus can indicate underlying psychological distress. The symptoms are faintness or dizziness, pains in the heart or chest, nausea or upset stomach, trouble getting one's breath, numbness or tingling in parts of the body, and feeling weak in parts of the body.

The second scale is Depression (DEP) and looks for core symptoms of clinical depression including feeling lonely, feeling blue, having no interest in things, feeling worthless, feeling hopeless about the future, and having thoughts of ending one's life.

The third scale is Anxiety (ANX), which looks for the presence of symptoms most often associated with anxiety. These include feeling nervous or shaky inside, feeling tense or keyed up, feeling fearful or suddenly scared for no reason, experiencing spells of terror or panic, and feeling extremely restless.

The Global Severity Index (GSI) is a summary of the previous three scales that Derogatis describes as "the single best indicator of the respondent's overall emotional adjustment or psychopathologic status."[3]

It is fortuitous that the BSI-18 was also given to the priest-respondents in the 2009 survey. Thus, we can longitudinally compare the 2021 scores with the 2009 scores. The results for our 2021 sample, the previous 2009 sample, and the norm sample of adult males in the United States are all reported in table 5.1.

Table 5.1. BSI-18 pathology results

	Priests, 2009	Priests, 2021	Gen. Male Pop.
BSI Somatization scale	48.89	48.84	50
BSI Depression scale	48.95	51.53	50
BSI Anxiety scale	47.48	48.35	50
BSI Global Severity Index	49.11	50.13	50

Note: BSI scales are calibrated as T-scores; thus the mean for the sample group of males is 50 and the standard deviation is 10.

The scores in table 5.1 are not percentages but rather T-scores: a T-score mean is calibrated to be 50 with 10 as one standard deviation. The priests' mean T-scores for the 2009 study and the 2021 study are almost equal. These results suggest that priestly psychological wellness remains fairly stable and likely slightly better than that of the general population of males in the United States. The norms for the general population were developed prior to the pandemic.

A number of emerging studies show a marked rise in the levels of anxiety and depression in the United States during the pandemic. For example, the US Census Bureau found during December 2020, the same time frame as our study, that 27.9% of US males reported symptoms of a depressive disorder, 32.2% reported symptoms of an anxiety disorder, and 37.9% reported symptoms of either an anxiety disorder or depressive disorder. The researchers compared that rate with a strikingly lower 2019 prepandemic rate (all adult males 18 years or older), with 6.5% reporting symptoms of a depressive disorder, 8.1% with symptoms of an anxiety disorder, and 10.8% with symptoms of either a depressive or anxiety disorder.[4] This is a fourfold increase in the general population!

Priestly Depression Rates Double in Pandemic

For the priests, the modest rise in the Depression scale from 2009 to 2021 was clearly visible from a T-score of 48.95 to 51.53. This, in turn, raised the Global Severity Index since the latter is simply the result of adding the raw scores of the three subscales. So the question ought to be raised, *Were priests more depressed in the midst of the COVID-19 pandemic?*

While the mean score rose modestly, the individual scores between the two groups differed significantly. In 2009, 7.5% of the priests' scores on the Depression scale fell into what the test developer called "caseness," that is, a T-score of 63 or higher. This suggests that these individuals had a significant level of depression that might even be diagnosable. These prepandemic levels are very similar to those reported in the general population by the aforementioned US Census Bureau findings. So priests' prepandemic mental health in general appeared to be roughly similar to that of their lay peers.

However, when the pandemic hit, there was a major difference. In 2021, the figure of depression in priests almost doubled to 14.5%. As one priest wrote on his survey, "What I've experienced during this time of pandemic is chronic fatigue and exhaustion." This clear rise in depression among priests should be a serious concern for the Church in general and priests in particular. Twice as many priests appear to be depressed during the pandemic. But the initial data suggest that this is much less of a rise than in the general population. The general population went from about 6.5% to 27.9%, a fourfold increase as noted previously by the US Census Bureau, while priest rates doubled.

Similarly, the percentage of priests with significant symptoms of anxiety (as measured by a T-score of 63 or greater) rose from 6.4% in a prepandemic 2009 to 9.3% in the midst of the pandemic in 2021. While not as great a rise as the rate of depression, it is of note. Again, this is much less of a rise than that experienced among laypeople. The laity went from 8.1% in 2019 to 32.2% in December of 2020. So, the rise in depression and anxiety among priests was considerably less.

While their mental health appears largely stable and slightly better than that of the general population, priests were not immune to deleterious psychological effects of the pandemic. Nevertheless, as a group they appeared to be less psychologically distressed by the pandemic than laypeople. It appears that mental health resilience in a crisis is greater among priests than their lay counterparts. This study will investigate some of the possible reasons for priestly resilience in a crisis.

PRIESTHOOD AND SUICIDALITY

Sad to say, on August 30, 2021, in the Diocese of Baton Rouge, a priest took his own life. He had long suffered from anxiety and depression.[5] It is possible that the added stress of the pandemic made it too difficult for him to cope.

The BSI-18 asks the respondents how much certain problems have distressed or bothered them recently, and one of the items listed is, "Thoughts of ending your life." In 2009, 0.2% of the priests said they were "quite a bit" or "extremely" bothered by suicidal thoughts. This number rose to 0.9% in 2021. While the overall percentages of suicidal ideation among priests remain very low, one suicide is one too many.

In an attempt to predict suicidality among priests, the variables in this survey were correlated with the above BSI-18 item.

The variables that significantly correlated with suicidal ideation are listed in table 5.2.

The BSI-18 scales of psychological health most strongly predicted feelings of suicidality. Inner feelings of distress—somatization, depression, and anxiety—plus the ProQOL 5 Burnout scale are most strongly predictive of suicidal ideation. Individuals who suffer negative inner states of depression, anxiety, and burnout are at increased risk for suicidal ideation.

It might be natural to assume that one's positive religious beliefs would be a deterrent to suicidality. Thus, the item "Thoughts of ending your life" was correlated with the ProQOL 5 item "I have beliefs that sustain me." It is a bit surprising that the correlation, while being statistically significant at the .001 level, was only $r = -.18$. So a priest's religious beliefs are likely a deterrent to suicidal ideation but are not a strong factor.

Table 5.2. The 2021 Pearson's _r_ correlations with BSI-18 item "Thoughts of ending your life"

BSI-18 Depression scale	.47
BSI-18 General Severity Index	.43
BSI-18 Anxiety scale	.35
ProQOL 5 Burnout scale	.27
BSI-18 Somatization scale	.25
"The abuse crisis has negatively impacted my faith"	.23
"I feel a sense of inner peace"	-.22
"I have a good self-image"	-.22
"The abuse crisis has negatively impacted my emotional well-being"	.21
"I suffer from loneliness"	.20
"I have beliefs that sustain me"	-.18

Note: All correlations are two-tailed and significant at the .01 level.

My own clinical experience in working with suicidal clients supports this. When people are suicidal, it is not a rational process. One's beliefs or nonbeliefs can affect one's state of mind, but the primary impetus to suicidal ideation is not an intellectual process but an emotional one. People frequently become suicidal, in my experience, in the wake of intense internal emotional distress, especially as a result of depression. Hence the strong correlation with the BSI-18 Depression scale. In fact, the variable "I have beliefs that sustain me" is actually one of the items that make up the Depression scale. So it is widely, and I think properly, held that depression and suicidality can be part of the same psychological dynamic.

As I often teach my students, if a person becomes depressed enough, he or she will consider suicide. In one case, a person was admonished by a fervent Christian not to end her life by suicide because she would "go to hell." The individual responded, "I am already in hell."

These reflections are supported by Ryan E. Lawrence and colleagues' review of the literature on religious beliefs and suicidality. They found that religious beliefs did not stop suicidal ideation but apparently reduced actual suicide attempts.[6] This is an important distinction. Similar to my findings and experience, suicidal ideation arises spontaneously in the wake of intense internal distress. Whether one acts upon that suicidal ideation and attempts to end one's life may be somewhat deterred by personal religious beliefs. As an example, one of my clients revealed to me that she was suicidal but then added, "I would not commit suicide because of my faith."

Other risk factors for suicidality also surfaced in this study. Priests who reported having a low self-image ($r = -.22$) and lacking a sense of inner peace ($r = -.22$) were more likely to be afflicted with thoughts of suicide. These might be considered more long-term, enduring personality difficulties and likely traceable back to childhood. In fact, the correlations between "Growing up, I suffered from anxiety and/or depression" and inner peace ($r = -.21$) and self-image ($r = -.29$) were modest but statistically significant ($p < .01$). While not accounting for all of what predicts adulthood problems with self-image and inner peace, childhood dysfunction clearly contributes to later problems. This again argues in favor of the current practice of psychologically screening candidates for the priesthood. Those with severe childhood trauma and dysfunction are at risk for developing psychological difficulties later in priesthood.

These findings that connect suicidality with underlying emotional distress have important pastoral consequences. Religious organizations—in fact, any organization— should pay close attention to members who are seriously anxious or depressed. Every attempt should be made not to stigmatize such individuals. And psychotherapeutic assistance should be made available swiftly. Working with depressed and anxious priests, I have found that many of them return to more normal functioning with early intervention, often quickly.

One priest wrote on his survey: "I am grateful to the diocese for paying for my therapy for many years with the same therapist. In therapy I have been able to integrate my sexuality into my celibacy over time. Priesthood has given me an identity to grow into."

BURNOUT IN PRIESTHOOD

Priest-respondents were given the ProQOL 5, which has three scales: Burnout, Compassion Satisfaction, and Secondary Traumatic Stress. Table 6.2 shows the resulting scores. The Burnout scale is composed of ten items measuring "exhaustion, frustration, anger and depression typical of burnout."[7] The Burnout scale survey results indicate that burnout rates for priests in the United States, as a whole, are low. The mean raw score on the scale is 19. This falls well within the "low" range (scores equal to or less than 22).

This mirrors the 2009 survey results using another measure of burnout, the Maslach Burnout Inventory (MBI). In the 2009 study, the mean MBI score for the priests in the sample was lower than that for the general population, suggesting a low level of burnout for priests in general. Of course, this does not mean there were no priests who were burned out. In 2009, about 2.3% scored in the high range of all three MBI subscales, indicating that a small percentage had a high degree of burnout.[8]

Examination of the individual scores in the 2021 study reveals that only two priests scored in the "high" range for the ProQOL 5 (raw score greater than or equal to 42). This is very low. However, there were 431 respondents (out of a usable 1,908 responses), or 23%, who scored in the "moderate" range of burnout. This was similar for the 2009 survey using the MBI Emotional Exhaustion scale: 22% scored in the "average" range. Such individuals are at moderate risk for burnout but likely do not currently have significant symptoms.

A number of written comments referred to the stress of priestly life and ministry, especially during the pandemic:

- "I think priests, and particularly pastors, are under a great deal of stress."

- "I think many of my answers are affected by the situation of lockdown—difficulty of normal parish and social contact during the pandemic."

- "Through the years the expectations keep growing and the support keeps decreasing."

- "Love being a priest but lots of stress."

- "My experience of priesthood has not always been easy, but it has been satisfying and has led to great joy."

The responses to the ProQOL 5 item "I feel overwhelmed because my case (work) load seems endless" illustrate this dynamic of some priests feeling overworked and stressed. See table 5.3.

Table 5.3. Results of 2021 survey: "I feel overwhelmed because my case (work) load seems endless"

Never (%)	Rarely (%)	Sometimes (%)	Often (%)	Very often (%)
19	37	32	9	4

In this 2021 sample, about 13% of priests say they often or very often feel overwhelmed by their heavy workloads. Frankly, this is not an unreasonable feeling in many priestly assignments today. I know more than a few priests who are running large parishes of well over 1,000 registered households plus serving a second smaller parish, as well as holding down an administrative position in the diocese. From 1970 to 2020, the number of Catholic priests in the United States decreased by more than 23,600 while the Catholic population rose by more than 18 million.[9] As one priest wrote on his survey: "I have more than two assignments/ministries. Too much!"

But as we have already noted, having too much work is not the same thing as being burned out. The MBI definition describes three aspects of burnout: a burned-out person typically feels emotionally spent or drained; they feel as if they are not accomplishing anything; and they are becoming emotionally callous or hardened toward those they help. Many of our priests have too much to do, and their workloads are increasing as the overall number of priests declines. But few fit the clinical criteria of actually being burned out. This suggests that they are surprisingly resilient in a time of stress. We will look at factors promoting resilience, which will help explain this finding.

In sum, consistent findings over a 12-year period, using two different samples and two different scales measuring burnout, found a low level of burnout among priests in the United States.

WHY IS BURNOUT SO LOW AMONG PRIESTS?

A number of variables were correlated to determine what is likely contributing to priests' emotional resilience to burnout during this stressful time. See table 5.4 for Pearson r correlations with the ProQOL 5 Burnout scale (strongest correlations listed first; all statistically significant $p < .001$).[10]

Table 5.4. Strongest correlations with ProQOL 5 Burnout scale

	r
Priestly happiness	-.65
Inner peace and self-image	-.60
Loneliness	.54
Relationship with God	-.54
Relationship with bishop	-.31
"Priests are supportive of each other"	-.31
"The Eucharist is the center of my life"	-.30
"I have good lay friends"	-.25
"Growing up, I suffered from anxiety and/or depression"	.28
"I feel competent to assist people suffering from trauma"	-.26
"As a child, I suffered from some trauma"	.24
"I have close priest friends"	-.21

$r^2 = .58$

When all of these variables were regressed together against the variable Burnout, the r squared = .58, which suggests that these variables account for 58% of the variance of burnout. This means they significantly account for more than half of what predicts burnout risk in these priests. This is a solid finding in social science research.

Many of these variables predicting burnout would, on the face of it, be expected, such as Priestly Happiness, Inner Peace, and Loneliness. However, there were three other variables I want to highlight that were important in predicting whether a priest would experience burnout:

- "Growing up, I suffered from anxiety and/or depression" (r = .28)
- "I feel competent to assist people suffering from trauma" (r = -.26)
- "As a child, I suffered from some trauma" (r = .24)

These findings are important. Adults who suffered traumas and psychological problems as children may be less successful in dealing with traumas as adults and more vulnerable to burnout.

In our sample of 1,962 priests from around the United States, 20% strongly agreed or agreed with the statement, "Growing up, I suffered from anxiety and/or depression," and 22% strongly agreed or agreed that "As a child, I suffered from some trauma." Thus, about one-fifth of priests agreed that in their childhood they were traumatized or suffered psychologically. While a minority, this is not an insignificant number. It is important for these individuals to deal with, and find some healing for, their childhood difficulties so that they can be of more help to others and not experience burnout themselves.

This finding suggests that another significant factor in reducing burnout is a priest's feeling of competency in handling the problems and difficulties that are part of his ministries. Training is important! When priests feel competent, especially in dealing with trauma, they are much less likely to burn out. Have we trained our priests in helping people with trauma?

In the priest sample, 80% of the respondents strongly agreed or agreed with the statement, "I feel competent to assist people suffering from trauma." While this is a good number, given the ongoing crises and tragedies affecting the American people, perhaps some additional training in ministering during a crisis would be helpful. Sadly, incidents of terrorism and violence are growing in the United States. Any diocese that has not yet experienced such incidents will do so in the not-too-distant future. I recommend that dioceses regularly train their priests and people in responding to trauma, crises, and violence.

At this point, it might also be helpful to say what does *not* strongly predict burnout. I have often heard in lectures that the way to forestall burning out is regular rest and exercise and taking time off from work. These are certainly good practices, but do they really affect burnout? The results in this 2021 study and in my 2009 research both suggest that the effect is small.

The Pearson's r correlation between the ProQOL 5 Burnout scale and "I take a day off each week" is statistically significant but only $r = -.13$. The correlation with Burnout and "I exercise on a regular basis" was a little stronger at $r = -.20$. Similarly in 2009, the correlation between the three MBI Burnout scales and the item "I take a day off per week" ranged from not significant to a small $r = -.10$. For the item "I exercise on a regular basis," the correlations were statistically significant but ranged only from $r = -.10$ to -.14.

In short, both studies demonstrate that regular exercise and rest, while likely helpful, do only a little to prevent burnout.

With the current emphasis on wellness in priestly formation, seminarians are strongly advised to develop healthy habits of rest and exercise in order not to burn out. While these are laudable practices, there are much more effective ways to prevent burnout. What ought to be impressed on seminarians is the importance of developing nourishing relationships, finding fulfillment in one's ministry, healing any internal psychic wounds, and sustaining a priestly spiritual life.

I would like to emphasize that the reported level of burnout among priests in the 2021 sample, as in the 2009 study, was low. To my mind, there is no doubt that many priests are overworked. But, as a group, they are not suffering from burnout. They are psychologically and spiritually sound and thus resilient in the face of considerable stress.

PSYCHOLOGICALLY DISTRESSED VS. HEALTHY PRIESTS

I have spent the majority of my years as a priest-psychologist working with suffering priests in particular. I thought it would be instructive to compare priests who scored the most psychologically distressed on the BSI-18 with those who scored the healthiest. The BSI-18 is a good overall measure of mental health and particularly captures those suffering from depression, anxiety, and somatization. Comparing those who are psychologically distressed with healthier individuals might render some insights into what makes a healthy priest.

Priests whose overall scores on the BSI-18 General Severity Index (BSI-GSI) were in the high or caseness range, above or equal to a T-score of 63, were compared with those who scored in a lower range, below or equal to a T-score of 37 (recall that the mean T-score is 50, which puts these two groups equidistant from the mean). That is, I compared those who scored in the high, psychologically distressed range with those who scored in the low, healthiest range. The essential research question is, *Are there any observable factors or traits from the research that can help predict a priest's mental health?* Once again, we must recall that correlations or descriptives from the data do not necessarily mean causation. We can draw on previous research and our own psychological and theological knowledge to infer such causal relationships.

Those with a T-score of 63 or above, in the distressed range, numbered 164 out of 1,691 valid test responses, or about 10%. These 164 respondents were the most psychologically distressed of the entire sample. Those with a T-score of 37 or less, in the healthiest range, numbered 277 out of 1,691, or about 16%. They were the least distressed of the entire sample. So, there are enough respondents in both the highest and lowest ranges to give us some statistically significant results.

DISTRESSED PRIESTS ARE LONELY

An examination of the data reveals a number of striking differences between the two groups.[11] Regarding friends and social connections, the healthier group reported a much stronger connection to others. That is, 65% strongly agreed to having close priest friends and 63% to having good lay friends, while the distressed group reported 40% and 41% respectively. The numbers for the distressed group are fully one third lower.

Clearly, healthy people are more strongly connected to others. Of the distressed group, only 6% strongly disagreed with the statement, "I suffer from loneliness," while a stunning 63%

of the healthiest group strongly disagreed and another 31% disagreed. This means that most of the distressed group said they were lonely and many were very lonely, while almost none of the healthy group said they were lonely. Perhaps this is one of the strongest traits and predictors of psychologically distressed clergy: they are lonely![12]

While modern seminaries in the United States typically emphasize the importance of healthy relationships for a healthy priesthood, I would like to make a case that more be done. Specifically, as previously noted, seminarians need to be trained in how to cultivate relationships. In this society, many seminarians come from one-child families or grew up in a somewhat socially isolated environment. Many do not know how to go about building relationships. In addition to stressing the need for relationships, we need to help them acquire the necessary tools to do so.

Much of the remedial work done in residential treatment centers for clergy focuses on building life-giving relationships, hence the importance of group therapy in a residential setting. Some residents from our therapy program reported making friends for the first time in their lives.

A DEGRADED SPIRITUAL LIFE

The spiritual lives of the psychologically distressed priests are also a cause for concern. Of the healthy group, 65% strongly agreed to having a good relationship with God, while only 29% of the distressed group did so. This is a large difference, less than half, and quite striking. Perhaps as a part of their internal distress, many of these priests feel estranged from God.

This is also reflected in their spiritual practices. Of the distressed group, 20% report praying privately fifteen minutes or fewer each day versus only 6% of the healthy group. Similarly,

36% of the healthy priests spend an hour or more in daily private prayer versus a much lower 20% of the distressed priests. So distressed priests, as a group, are praying less.

Forty-four percent of distressed priests say they have a spiritual director, as compared with 58% of the healthy group. The distressed group is also less likely to receive the Sacrament of Penance regularly (39% of the distressed group go at least monthly versus 48% of the healthy group), and they are less likely to make an annual retreat (83% versus 93%).

Another striking finding is the difference in Eucharistic spirituality. Of the healthy group, 79% strongly agreed with the statement, "The Eucharist is the center of my life," versus 49% for the distressed group. This difference is important and bears reflection. There is an intimate connection between the priesthood and the Eucharist, as noted consistently in Church teaching. For example, St. John Paul II wrote in his 2004 Holy Thursday letter to priests, "The ministerial priesthood . . . is born, lives, works and bears fruit 'de Eucharistia.'" Similarly, in an oft-quoted line from the Second Vatican Council's *Lumen Gentium*, "Eucharistic sacrifice is the source and summit of the Christian life."

The question naturally arises, *Are the decreased spiritual practices of the distressed priests a consequence of their internal dysphoria or a cause of it?* It is impossible to say definitively, but it is likely a mutual interaction. A lack of prayer and personal distress likely mutually influence and reinforce each other.

As a psychologist, I ministered in a psychological treatment program for clergy for two decades. An old 12-step adage is, "Spirituality is the first thing to go and the last thing to return." That is, a degradation in one's spiritual life typically precedes an overall decline in a person's mental health, and on the road to recovery, it is one of the last things to be healed and return.

It is not surprising that the distressed group reported much lower levels of happiness and much higher levels of considering leaving the priesthood. When given the statement, "My morale as a priest is good," only 13% of the distressed group strongly agreed, compared with 73% of the healthy group. Similarly, only one priest of the healthy group of 277 (0.4%) said he was thinking of leaving the priesthood versus 12% of the distressed group. It is clear that internal psychological distress is a very strong predictor of low morale and thoughts of leaving the ministry.

This is borne out by the Pearson's r correlations. The BSI-GSI, indicating the overall mental health of the respondent, is significantly correlated ($p < .001$) to Relationship with God ($r = -.31$), a Eucharistic spirituality ($r = -.21$), thoughts of leaving the ministry ($r = .32$), and especially one's morale ($r = -.47$). This affirms once again how critical it is for dioceses and religious orders to identify and assist priests who are suffering from internal distress, especially depression and anxiety. There is a very strong likelihood that such priests are isolated, unhappy, living a degraded spiritual life, and perhaps even thinking of leaving the ministry.

Moreover, these correlations highlight the importance of a strong spiritual life for the health and happiness of priests. Most Catholic dioceses in the United States have an annual gathering of their priests. Often there are speakers and talks on various topics. A conference focused on the priest's relationship with God and his spiritual life would be beneficial. It is a subject we often take for granted or feel is something private to the priest. However, the data suggest that a strong spiritual life and relationship with God are essential to the health of a priest's life and ministry. Shouldn't we focus more on this?

CHILDHOOD TRAUMA AND PRIESTHOOD

Having worked with many priests suffering from psychological and spiritual problems, I have become acutely aware of the negative impact of childhood trauma, especially if this trauma has not been addressed in a healing modality. The 2021 survey contained five statements related to childhood trauma and dysfunction:

- "Growing up, I had a good relationship with my mother."
- "Growing up, I had a good relationship with my father."
- "I grew up in a dysfunctional family."
- "Growing up, I suffered from anxiety and/or depression."
- "As a child, I suffered from some trauma."

The respondents were asked to what degree they concurred with each statement. Based upon solid statistical analysis, these statements were all combined to form one composite variable, which I named Childhood Trauma.[13]

When this variable was correlated with other major composite variables and T-tests were run comparing group means, it became clear that those who suffered from significant childhood trauma and dysfunction were less likely to be happy with self as an adult (Self-Esteem, $r = -.36$, $p < .001$), more likely to suffer psychologically (BSI-GSI, $r = .37$, $p < .001$), and less likely to be happy with priesthood (Priestly Happiness, $r = -32$, $p < .001$). (The variable Self-Esteem is a combination of two items on the survey: "I have a good self-image" and "I feel a sense of inner peace.")[14]

For example, when given the item "I like my work as a [helper]," 67% of those who did not suffer childhood trauma or dysfunction chose "very often," as opposed to 46% of those from the childhood trauma/dysfunction group.[15] Similarly, when presented with the statement, "I am the person I always wanted to be," 19% of those with childhood trauma/dysfunction chose "very often" compared with 40% of those without childhood trauma/dysfunction. On the item "I have a good self-image," 43% of those without childhood trauma/dysfunction strongly agreed, compared with only 15% of those with childhood trauma/dysfunction. Likewise, 39% of the childhood trauma/dysfunction group strongly agreed with the statement, "Overall, I am happy as a priest," compared with 72% of those without childhood trauma/dysfunction. T tests on each of these were highly significant ($p < .001$).

In a comparison of the priests' overall scores on the test of mental health (BSI-GSI), the T-score of the childhood trauma/dysfunction group was 54 compared to 46 for the group without childhood trauma/dysfunction. Recall that 50 is the mean for a T-score, so the group who had suffered from childhood trauma was psychologically less healthy than the mean compared to the other group. The group that did not suffer from childhood trauma was psychologically healthier than the mean.

We can conclude that those with a dysfunctional experience in childhood are much less likely to be happy in priesthood, less likely to be happy with self, and more likely to suffer from anxiety or depression as adults. Dioceses and religious orders are already psychologically screening candidates for the priesthood. They are doing a good job screening out those with major mental illness such as schizophrenia and other psychotic disorders. But lesser forms of childhood dysfunction, as we can see from this study, will likely have a significant impact on the priest's happiness and ultimately the fruitfulness of his ministry. Those with major dysfunction in their past are probably not suitable candidates, and those with lesser but significant levels of dysfunction should be heavily screened and healing remedies applied as needed before ordination.

HIGHER RATES OF ANXIETY AND DEPRESSION IN YOUNGER PRIESTS

Comparing the mental health scores of younger and older priests found that younger priests have higher rates of depression and anxiety. Figure 5.1 shows the mean of the BSI-18 T-scores of younger versus older priests on the measure of depression. For example, the T-score for priests ordained 1–10 years was 53.5, as compared with 50.6 for priests ordained 42–50 years.[16]

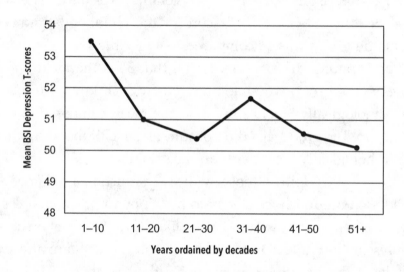

Figure 5.1. Depression scores by years ordained

Similarly, figure 5.2 compares the mean of the BSI-18 T-scores of younger and older priests on the measure of anxiety. Again, younger priests evidence higher levels of pathology. For example, the T-score for priests ordained 1–10 years was 50.5, as compared with 47.1 for priests ordained 41–50 years. While the overall differences in the rates of depression and anxiety were not large, they were statistically significant, suggesting that priests in their first ten years are somewhat more susceptible to symptoms of anxiety and depression.

Moreover, when looking at the percentage of priests by years ordained who are depressed (BSI-18 Depression T-score $\geq$ 63), the difference becomes more apparent. Of priests ordained 1–10 years, 19.3% scored in the depressed range, compared with 11% for the remainder of the priests. This is a remarkable difference: depression rates for the newly ordained were approaching twice those of other priests.

When looking at the percentage of priests by years ordained who suffer from anxiety (BSI-18 Anxiety T-score $\geq$ 63), we see an even greater difference. Of priests ordained 1–10 years, the anxiety rate was 13.6%, compared with 6.6% for the rest of the priests. This rate of anxiety for the newly ordained is more than double that of other priests! Thus younger priests had significantly higher rates of both depression and anxiety.

Figure 5.2. Anxiety scores by years ordained

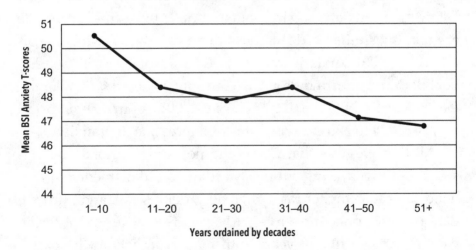

How can we account for the higher rates of depression and anxiety among younger priests? Were they psychologically more vulnerable to the two crises? Did their age cohort have higher rates of depression and anxiety in general? Or is it perhaps just a factor of their adjusting to priesthood? As we shall see in chapter 9, younger priests were not traumatized more than older priests as a result of the two crises. Moreover, on the variable Childhood Trauma, which was composed of five items measuring trauma in childhood, younger priests did not report greater childhood trauma than the older priests.

Similarly, the ProQOL 5 Burnout scale shows that younger priests scored highest on measures of burnout. See figure 5.3. Burnout scores slowly decreased as priests aged in ministry. Burnout is likely a function not only of those variables previously mentioned, but also of how new a priest is in ministry. This finding confirms my 2009 study using the Maslach Burnout Inventory. Again, the newly ordained scored highest on the Burnout scale.[17]

Visual inspection shows that the trajectory of the scores on Depression, Anxiety, and Burnout for priests by ordination decade are roughly similar. Indeed, these three variables are highly correlated. For BSI Anxiety and ProQOL 5 Burnout, $r = .56$, $p < .001$. For BSI Depression and ProQOL 5 Burnout, $r = .65$, $p < .001$. For BSI Depression and BSI Anxiety, $r = .68$, $p < .001$. A burned-out priest is very likely to exhibit symptoms of depression and anxiety.

All this suggests that we should not underestimate the personal challenges facing our newly ordained. Adjustment to priesthood can cause higher rates of anxiety, depression, and burnout. One priest-respondent wrote: "My first few years of pastoring were my most difficult years with many conflicts in the parish and limited experience to draw upon. Today those similar types of conflicts do not have the kind of impact on me as in the past."

Another priest commented, "The transition from seminary to ordained ministry was so stark. I really struggled going from a community experience to living in a rectory with one person."

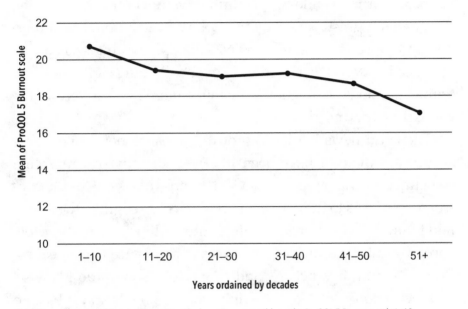

Figure 5.3. ProQOL 5 Burnout scale by ordination decade

Note: The y-axis starts at 10 and not zero since the lowest score possible on the ProQOL 5 Burnout scale is 10.

Many dioceses have special programs to assist the newly ordained, including regular meetings in support groups. This study affirms the need for such programs and suggests all dioceses should have something in place for the newly ordained.

PSYCHOTHERAPY FOR PRIESTS

It is important to note that 39% of the entire sample of 1,962 priests reported to have been in psychotherapy or counseling sometime during their priesthood. In the 2009 survey, it was 46% of priests. Overall, this is an encouraging statistic; psychological services are apparently readily available to most priests, and many avail themselves of this kind of help.

It is not surprising that of priests who suffered from childhood trauma/dysfunction, 72% report having been in counseling sometime during their priesthood. This is compared with only 28% of those without childhood trauma/dysfunction. The question did not distinguish between those who privately sought out therapy and those for whom ecclesiastical superiors intervened and requested it. Nevertheless, this is an encouraging sign that those with childhood dysfunction were much more likely to receive the counseling they needed.

The good news is that 39% of the priest-respondents in this survey affirmed, "I have been in psychotherapy or counseling sometime during my priesthood." Perhaps this is one of the contributing factors to the overall psychological strength of the priesthood. As a part of clinical training, future clinicians are typically encouraged to find their own sources of assistance when needed. Priests, as frontline helpers and counselors, should do likewise, and many do. They, too, are helping professionals and subject to significant stresses when assisting others who are suffering from trauma. As one priest-respondent wrote: "I have known anxiety and depression in the past. With proper medication and direction, I am no longer anxious or depressed. Praise God!"

6

TWO CRISES AND THEIR EFFECTS ON PRIESTS

The two crises currently affecting the Catholic Church in the United States, the sexual abuse crisis and the pandemic, have been devastating to many priests and laypeople alike. Certainly, there have to be measurable effects on the priests themselves. This study sought to research some of those effects and recommend healing measures for the future.

PANDEMIC ECLIPSING ABUSE CRISIS

Perhaps the best place to start when assessing the effects of these two crises on priests is simply to ask the priests themselves. I put the question to them directly: Have these crises affected you personally? In table 6.1, we see their responses.

Table 6.1. Results of 2021 survey: The abuse crisis vs. the COVID-19 pandemic

	Strongly agree (%)	Agree (%)	Unsure (%)	Disagree (%)	Strongly disagree (%)
"The abuse crisis has negatively affected my emotional well-being"	2.7	16.1	13.2	43.0	25.0
"The COVID-19 pandemic has been traumatic for me personally"	6.8	24.6	14.5	36.0	18.1

While the wording of the two survey items is not identical, both items attempt to assess if the respondents feel these two crises have negatively affected them. The COVID-19 statement is a bit stronger, using the word "traumatic" versus "negatively affected." Despite the stronger statement, it appears that more priests were being negatively affected by the pandemic at the time of the survey (31% strongly agreed or agreed) compared with the abuse crisis (19% strongly agreed or agreed); the latter was waning from public scrutiny. As the 2012 CARA study found regarding the abuse crisis, "Priests felt horror and sadness for victims, anger at diocesan and religious order administrators, and shock at the scope of the problem. Most priests are not preoccupied by such emotions today, although pain lingers for some."[1]

My experience working with priests supports this finding. In the midst of the pandemic, priests were typically more concerned about it than the abuse crisis. Some of the priest-respondents directly commented on the effects of the pandemic:

- "My negative emotions and perspective only surfaced during the pandemic when I was constantly exposed to death and sickness."

- "The COVID pandemic has cut our parish attendees in half. While we are seeing some slow return, I fear most will not come back. COVID has also taken a personal toll on the priests and staff. As a priest, I've had only 8 days of vacation in 17 months and zero weekends off."

Nevertheless, it is important to recognize that almost 19% of priests still say the abuse crisis has negatively affected their well-being. Some of the priest-respondents commented directly on the negative impact of the abuse crisis:

- "Having a brother step away from active ministry [because of an abuse allegation] has been very difficult these last few months."

- "The sexual abuse crisis has been a major determining factor in my day. It makes me feel betrayed because it was always going on. The fact that I didn't realize how bad this situation was makes me ashamed of myself. I feel I've wasted my life."

- "I feel the abuse crisis has negatively affected me and many other priests. . . . I would not encourage a young man to go into the priesthood."

Thus, for some, the abuse crisis has had a major impact. As noted above, one priest said it made him feel that he has "wasted" his life; a second priest would no longer encourage priestly vocations.

Regarding the pandemic, an important question was whether priests felt they were receiving sufficient assistance in the midst of the crisis. In response to the item "I feel overwhelmed by the COVID-19 pandemic and need more support," only 3% strongly agreed and 11% agreed. So the large majority of priests felt they were coping and were getting the support they needed. This does not, however, mitigate the personal distress many priests were feeling in the midst of the crisis.

On the other hand, a few priests commented on how the pandemic had, at least in part, been a personal blessing:

- "COVID-19 was a blessing insofar as it slowed my life down."

- "This pandemic has given me opportunities to develop some of my hidden talents and strengthen my faith and commitment as a servant of God."

ARE PRIESTS SUFFERING SECONDARY TRAUMA?

It is sometimes said that there is a high rate of burnout in priesthood. Indeed, there are a number of very real factors in the life of a priest that might lead one to believe it:

- Long hours

- A flood of unsolvable needs

- Intense work and relentless responsibilities

- Lack of appreciation by parishioners and other laypeople

- Compassion fatigue, a possible consequence of working with suffering people

- Never-ending public shaming with regard to the sexual abuse crisis

Given these intense factors, plus the current two crises, one might hypothesize that priests, as a group, are likely suffering from secondary traumatic stress as well as burnout. As noted previously, while some priests are experiencing burnout, the overall rate of burnout among US priests is low. Their mean raw score on the Burnout scale was 19. Scores below 22 are in the lower 25% and are considered low.

The ProQOL 5 also measures secondary traumatic stress (STS). This is the stress on the caregiver when ministering to those who are undergoing trauma. The ProQOL manual describes the STS scale: "STS is about work-related, secondary exposure to people who have experienced extremely or traumatically stressful events. The negative effects of STS may include fear, sleep difficulties, intrusive images, or avoiding reminders of the person's traumatic experiences."[2]

Are priests suffering from a moderate to high level of secondary traumatic stress as a result of working with traumatized people, particularly in the wake of the abuse crisis and in the midst of the pandemic? The results suggest that, as a group, they are not. Their mean raw score on the STS scale was 20, which falls in the low range (22 or below). See table 6.2.

Next, I looked at individual scores of the 1,962 priests in the sample. The individual priests in the sample who fell in the "high" category of secondary trauma numbered 0.3% (raw score above 42), which is a very small number. Most of the priests (71%) fell in the "low" range, with the remainder falling in the "moderate" range. There were no significant differences between the scores of younger and older priests.

Table 6.2. The 2021 ProQOL 5 scores

	All Priests, 2021 (N = 1,962)	
Compassion Satisfaction (CS)	42	High Upper 25%
Burnout (BO)	19	Low Lower 25%
Secondary Traumatic Stress (STS)	20	Low Lower 25%

Note: These are raw scores, not percentages.

I do not want to lightly dismiss scores in the "moderate" range (raw score of 23–42); 29% of the priests scored in this range. For example, 2% of the priests responded "very often" or "often" to the item "I feel depressed because of the traumatic experiences of the people I help." While this is a relatively small number, it does suggest that a percentage of priests were psychologically suffering while helping others in the crisis.

Helping these priests learn how to support others in a way that does not harm themselves is important. Perhaps workshops teaching the difference between being empathetic and sympathetic—helping others compassionately without taking on their pain—would be useful. Mentoring by a senior priest might also be helpful, the mentors being chosen, at least partly, for their wisdom and pastoral balance.

The overall positive results of this portion of the survey do not mean that these crises have not been difficult. A number of priests noted that the events surrounding these crises have been stressful, and many report feeling negative psychological effects. But priests appear to have considerable resilience and the tools to deal with such trauma. On the other side of the pandemic, most priests will not likely suffer long-term traumatic symptoms as a result. But a few will.

TRUST IN BISHOPS DECLINES

While the abuse crisis does not appear to be causing serious psychological trauma in most priests, it may be having negative effects in other areas. For example, it has been reported that the abuse crisis has shaken people's trust in Church leadership, in the priesthood, and perhaps even in the faith. So, I posed this question to priests directly: Has the abuse crisis negatively affected your view of Church leadership, the priesthood, or the faith? Table 6.3 gives the results.

Table 6.3. Results of 2021 survey: Priests' negative perceptions as a result of the abuse crisis

	Strongly agree (%)	Agree (%)	Unsure (%)	Disagree (%)	Strongly disagree (%)
"The abuse crisis has negatively impacted my faith"	2.4	5.7	6.5	36.2	49.2
"The abuse crisis has negatively impacted my view of the priesthood"	6.6	22.3	9.3	33.4	28.4
"The abuse crisis has negatively impacted my view of Church leadership"	21.7	33.5	11.8	20.9	12.1

As we see in table 6.3, the vast majority of priests are not reporting that the abuse crisis affected their faith. They distinguished between what errant priests and bishops do versus the faith itself. However, there were still 8% of priests who reported a negative effect on their faith, which is not insignificant. If the abuse crisis has shaken the faith of 8% of our priests, it is not something to be ignored.

A larger effect is on priests' perception of the priesthood in general. Fully 29% agreed or strongly agreed that the abuse crisis has negatively affected their view of priesthood. While still a minority, this is a substantial figure. The abuse crisis has soiled the perceptions of many priests of the very institution to which they belong. How can such a negative impact be repaired? This ought to be a cause for concern and reflection.

What was most striking was the response to the third item, "The abuse crisis has negatively impacted my view of Church leadership." A majority, 55%, strongly agreed or agreed with this statement. The abuse crisis has most strongly affected priests' views of Church leadership. This should not be surprising since the focus of media attention was on the perceived poor handling of abuse cases, ranging from charges of incompetence to outright deceit and corruption. The abuse crisis has measurably damaged the reputation of US Catholic bishops among priests (and certainly the people as well).

WHAT AFFECTS THE DECLINE IN TRUST IN BISHOPS?

What might be a more surprising statistic, given the onslaught of criticism of the leadership of the Catholic Church, is that one third of priest-respondents said that the crisis has *not* affected their view of Church leadership. I decided to compare the two groups: those who said the crisis did affect their view of bishops and those who said it did not. Were there any noticeable differences between the two groups?

I first ran a T test to see if the two groups were statistically different on any of the variables. Then I ran a Pearson's *r* correlation on the item variable "The abuse crisis has negatively impacted my view of Church leadership" and these variables to get a sense of the strength of the item's effect. (Once again, let me remind the reader that correlation does not mean causation. Thus, one is always cautious about which variables are the cause and which are the effect. It is likely in social science research that the variables are mutually reinforcing.)

The most significant variables fell into three general categories: underlying psychological wholeness, current mental health, and current relationship to the bishop.[3] Regarding the first, underlying psychological wholeness, those who had a more stable psychological background were less likely to have a degraded perception of Church leadership in the wake of the abuse crisis. "I feel a sense of inner peace" ($r = -.25$), "I have a good self-image" ($r = -.22$), and the previously noted composite variable Childhood Trauma composed of five items ($r = .26$) all correlated significantly with "The abuse crisis has negatively impacted my view of Church leadership."

Thus, those with underlying psychological wounds and weaknesses were more likely to feel a psychic wound toward Church leadership in the wake of the public scandals. Past wounds and underlying weaknesses appear to be a vulnerability. Past wounds likely make one more susceptible to wounds in the present. If these wounds are not healed, current traumas can pull off the "psychic scab" and the person experiences, once again, the trauma of childhood hurts, which compounds the pain of current crises.

Regarding the second category, measures of current mental health correlated significantly with "The abuse crisis has negatively impacted my view of Church leadership": ProQOL Burnout scale ($r = .32$), BSI Depression ($r = .31$), BSI Anxiety ($r = .23$), BSI Global Severity Index ($r = .30$). Thus, priests who were suffering psychologically due to symptoms of depression, anxiety, and/or burnout were more likely to have more negative views of Church leadership in the wake of the abuse crisis. Like background psychological variables, one's current mental state, if in a place of vulnerability and distress, is more likely to be affected by negative news and valuations of one's leadership. These variables can be mutually reinforcing: as one's trust in Church leadership declines, it can negatively influence a priest's psychic state, perhaps exacerbating symptoms of depression, anxiety, and burnout.

But the variables that most strongly predicted how the abuse scandal would negatively affect one's view of Church leadership were the two items directly related to one's bishop: "I support my bishop's leadership" (r = -.35) and "I have a good relationship with my bishop" (r = -.38). At first glance, this might seem obvious, and one might ask if it really tells us anything. In reality, I think it tells us something very important. Those who had a good relationship with their bishop were much more likely to take the abuse scandal in stride and not let it affect their underlying view of Church leadership as much. But without such a strong relationship, priests are more easily swayed by public events. This reaffirms the importance of the relationship between priests and their bishop for the ongoing well-being of the presbyterate.

PRIESTS' RELATIONSHIPS WITH THEIR BISHOPS

Given the importance of the relationship between priests and their bishops, I wanted to compare over three surveys (2004, 2009, 2021) the responses of priests on their self-reported relationship with their bishop. The results are interesting and important. See table 6.4.

Table 6.4. Results of 2004, 2009, and 2021 surveys: "I have a good relationship with my bishop"

	Strongly agree (%)	Agree (%)	Unsure (%)	Disagree (%)	Strongly disagree (%)
2004 survey	16.7	58.2	15.3	6.9	2.9
2009 survey	26.1	50.5	16.6	4.5	2.3
2021 survey	27.9	45.5	16.9	5.9	3.9

First, it should be noted that priests' perception of their relationship with their bishops has been relatively stable over this 17-year period, despite ongoing sexual abuse scandals. In fact, not only have their relationships not gotten worse, but the data suggest that in some regards the relationships have slightly improved! In 2004, 16.7% strongly agreed (and 58.2% agreed) that they had a good relationship with their bishop, while in 2009, 26.1% strongly agreed (50.5% agreed) and in 2021, 27.9% strongly agreed (45.5% agreed). The percentage of those who feel more estranged from their bishop remains stable during this 17-year period at about 7 to 9%.

Is that "approval" rating good or bad? This is not exactly an approval rating, such as an employee rating one's boss from a distance. Rather, it is a more personal variable. A point of reference might be a comparison with industry surveys on CEO approval ratings. In a July 2016 Glassdoor study of over 70,000 employees, the highest CEO approval ratings were in the real estate industry at 76% and the lowest came from retail at 61.4%.[4] Our data suggest that US bishops compare very favorably; 73–77% of priests strongly agree or agree that their relationship with their bishop is good.

But a word of caution is in order. The relationship between a priest and his bishop is typically more complex, multilayered, and personally impactful than that of a secular employee to the boss. No company would dare insist that its employees, upon joining the company, kneel in front of the CEO, put their hands in the CEO's hands, and promise obedience to the CEO and successors. But this is precisely what a priest does. The implications of such a sacred and solemn promise are deep and immense. If one quarter of priests do not feel they have a good relationship with their bishop or are unsure, bishops ought to take note and begin a process of reflection: Why is that? What can and should I do?

This data might seem to contradict the earlier finding that 55% of priests said that the abuse crisis had negatively affected their relationship with Church leadership. If so, why hasn't their relationship with their own bishop suffered more? It appears that priests' relationship with their own bishops is staying fairly stable and relatively strong.

I offer the following conjecture; readers are welcome to offer their own. There can be a difference between how a priest feels toward bishops in general and how he feels toward his own bishop in particular. It reminds me of what someone told me about lawyers: "I hate lawyers, but I like my own lawyer." I suspect many people would say today, "I don't like bishops; but I like my bishop." It is one thing to disdain an abstract group at a distance (i.e., bishops); it is another to like or dislike the bishop in one's own diocese. Our feelings toward bishops as a whole are likely to be much more affected by public statements and media. Our feelings toward our own bishop are more likely affected by our personal interactions with the bishop over several years. In these days of public denigration of bishops, and given the critical and sacred nature of the bond between a bishop and his priests, it behooves individual bishops to spend time with and foster solid connections with their priests. It ought to be a high priority of every bishop.

A Pandemic of Loneliness

As noted previously, depression rates among priests rose during the pandemic. The results of the BSI-18 suggest that depression rates among priests doubled from 7.5% in 2009 to 14.5% in 2021. However, rates of depression in the general population increased almost fourfold during the pandemic. So, relatively speaking, the deleterious psychological effects seem to be less for priests than for the general population.

A closer look at the BSI-18 Depression scale reveals which items were most elevated for the priests who scored in the distressed range in 2021. Of the six items measuring depression, the one that was clearly most elevated was "Feeling lonely." A large 52% of priests who scored in the depressed range indicated that in the last seven days, they had felt lonely "quite a bit" or "extremely." Moreover, they were aware that they were suffering from loneliness. When given the additional statement, "I suffer from loneliness," fully 62% of those who scored in the depressed range strongly agreed or agreed.

Of the 1,141 priests who were not in the clinical range of the Depression scale (BSI Depression T-score ≤ 50), not one chose "quite a bit" or "extremely" in response to the item "Feeling lonely," as opposed to 52% of the depressed group. Similarly, only 8% of the group who were not depressed strongly agreed or agreed that they suffered from loneliness versus 62% of the depressed group. This is a very large difference.

We might conclude that when priests get depressed, one of the strongest symptoms of their depression is loneliness. It is a strong marker of a priest at risk for depression. Moreover, since depression rates of priests doubled during the pandemic, we might conclude that it was a pandemic of loneliness for depressed priests.

Loneliness was likely one of the greatest trials for all priests and, in fact, for the general population during the pandemic. Stores were closed. Travel was limited. People often had to wear face coverings. Many churches were closed. People were isolated inside their apartments and houses. So, too, for priests. Their congregations were gone. Their daily interactions with their parishioners dried up. Masses were often said privately or telecast via Zoom. Priests, too, were isolated. For some priests, this was very difficult. As one priest wrote on his survey: "COVID has taken its toll on me. Without contact with people, something integral is missing."

A celibate priest is a man for the people. In our survey, 96% of respondents reported having good lay friends. While the priest is meant to be a source of spiritual support for the people, the reverse is also true: the people are a great source of support for the priest. In the pandemic, this critical source of support was minimal and, at times, nonexistent. It is little wonder that some priests felt lonely and even depressed.

To me, these findings are quite striking. Loneliness is a critical factor in the psychological health of priests. It ought to be a strong consideration for any efforts to promote the welfare of priests.

7

THE RELATIONAL LIVES OF PRIESTS

G iven the data so far in this study, one would expect that loneliness in priesthood would negatively correlate with items reporting good relationships with other priests and with the laity. It would only make sense that priests who report having strong interpersonal relationships would be healthier and happier, and less lonely. What do the data actually show?

I combined the two items "I have close priest friends" and "I have good lay friends."[1] This new variable, titled Interpersonal Relationships, measures a priest's perceived relationship with other people—laity and other priests. I then correlated this variable with variables measuring psychological wellness and happiness. Did the connection pan out as hypothesized?

The answer is clearly yes. The variable Interpersonal Relationships was significantly correlated with measures of psychological wellness: the BSI Global Severity Index ($r = -.22$), BSI Depression scale ($r = -.25$), and ProQOL 5 Burnout scale ($r = -.27$). All were statistically significant ($p < .001$). Priests who report having good relationships with other priests and the laity had higher levels of mental health with less depression and burnout.

The variable Interpersonal Relationships was also significantly correlated ($p < .001$) with measures of happiness in priestly life and ministry: "Overall I am happy as a priest" ($r = .31$), "My morale as a priest is good" ($r = .30$), and ProQOL 5 Compassion Satisfaction scale ($r = .30$). Not surprisingly, having good relationships was positively correlated with two specific items from the ProQOL 5 measuring happiness with ministry: "My work makes me feel satisfied" ($r = .24$) and "I am happy that I chose to do this work" ($r = .24$).

Priesthood is a "people" job. Learning theology and the rules of ministry is critical. But a happy priest must also connect well with other people. Ultimately, the bond between the priest and his people greatly enhances the success of his ministry. He is their pastor and their shepherd. The time the priest spends getting to know his people and their getting to know him is time well spent. This again drives home the importance of a priest developing good relational skills—for his own health and happiness as well as for an effective ministry.

NINETY PERCENT OF PRIESTS HAVE GOOD RELATIONSHIPS

In the midst of the pandemic, how did priests do in regard to their relationships? We have seen how important strong interpersonal relationships are for their psychological health and happiness. Did the pandemic have a negative impact on their relations? Certainly, the restrictions imposed by COVID-19 safety precautions made connections more difficult. As one priest wrote: "The inability to socialize with lay friends during the COVID pandemic is a painful deprivation."

The BSI-18 asks respondents how they have felt in the last thirty days. One item specifically asked about loneliness. In 2009, 9% of the sample of priests said they experienced feeling lonely "quite a bit" or "extremely," and 76% said they experienced feeling lonely "not at all" or "a little bit." This same item was included in the 2021 survey and thus can be compared with the 2009 results. In 2021, the percentage of priest-respondents who said they experienced feeling lonely "quite a bit" or "extremely" actually decreased from 9% to 5%, and the percentage who said they experienced feeling lonely "not at all" or "a little bit" rose from 76% to 83%. So the self-reported experience of loneliness actually decreased slightly from 2009 to 2021.

In the midst of the pandemic, then, priests reported a slightly lesser degree of loneliness than they did before the pandemic. I suspect that priests answered this question based upon their over-all experience beyond the pandemic. They realized that the inter-personal isolation of the crisis was temporary. Such temporary pauses do not obviate one's good relationships and may actually help people to value them more.

It is also helpful to place this finding in the broader context of the health and wellness of priests. The mental health of priests, as measured by the BSI-18, remained fairly stable from 2009 to 2021, despite the abuse crisis and the pandemic. As a group, priests continue to display considerable stability and resilience in the face of these challenges.

Looking at priests' interpersonal relationships should give us additional insights. The item "I have close priest friends" was included in both the 2009 and 2021 surveys. In 2009, 88% strongly agreed or agreed with the statement, as compared with 91% in 2021. So the percentage of priests reporting good relationships with other priests actually increased somewhat.

Similarly, in 2009, the respondents were given the statement, "I have good lay friends who are an emotional support for me personally." A solid 93% strongly agreed or agreed with this statement. In 2021, 96% strongly agreed or agreed with a similar statement, "I have good lay friends." Again, this is actually a modest increase. One priest wrote on his survey: "At 95, I can't help people much. They help me. I had wonderful parishes to serve. The faithful sustained me."

The interpersonal relational lives of priests appear to be getting slightly stronger, despite the challenges of COVID-19. In fact, this is clearly one of the great strengths of more than 90% of priests—their ability to form and maintain good relationships with other priests and with laity. When we look at the factors for resilience in the face of crises in priesthood later in this work, this no doubt will be an important contributor to resilience.

PRIESTS ARE LESS LONELY THAN THE LAITY

In May 2021, around the same time period as our priest survey, the American Perspectives Survey conducted by the Survey Center on American Life sampled 2,019 adults in the United States. The survey found that relationships among adults are declining. Specifically, "Americans report having fewer close friendships than they once did, talking to their friends less often, and relying less on their friends for personal support." A large 49% of Americans say they have three or fewer close friends. Only 51% report that they are very or completely satisfied with the number of friends they have.[2]

These findings are similar to the results of Cigna's loneliness surveys. In 2018, Cigna concluded there was an epidemic of loneliness in the United States, with 54% of Americans reporting that they are lonely. Two years later, in January 2020, Cigna surveyed 10,400 adults and those numbers got even worse, with 61% now reporting feeling lonely. The rates were higher among men than women. The study noted the "increasing use of technology, more telecommuting and the always-on work culture

. . . are leaving Americans more stressed, less rested, spending more time on social media, and less time with friends and family."[3]

These rates of loneliness among the general population are much higher than those self-reported by priests. In our 2021 survey, 24% of priest-respondents indicated that they experience feeling lonely "moderately," "quite a bit," or "extremely." When given the item "I suffer from loneliness," 21% of priests strongly agreed or agreed. While these numbers are not insignificant and suggest that an offer of direct assistance to these priests is warranted, priests' level of loneliness appears relatively lower than that of the general population.

Nevertheless, the isolation of the pandemic has been difficult for many priests, as indicated in these survey responses:

- "I was ordained during COVID quarantine. Pandemic is all I've known as a priest. I can't wait to see whole faces, smiles, be able to shake hands and give hugs, and visit nursing homes. I think other priests and I would be happier if the masks and distancing were to go away. We need humanity back."

- "I moved during COVID. I am waiting to get to know the people [in the new assignment] and having them get to know me."

The sexual abuse crisis also has had a negative impact on some priests' relationships. One priest-respondent wrote: "The sexual abuse crisis has made it difficult for me to feel as close as I would like to people—especially women of my own age—as I am always second-guessing boundaries. It has made it difficult to be unguarded and to act 'natural.'"

Despite the very real challenges of the two crises, the majority of the presbyterate report having good relational lives. In recent years, negative assumptions are often made about priests based upon largely anecdotal data. For example, it is often assumed that priests are lonely because they do not have their own families. But when compared with loneliness rates among the laity, the data show that priests are much better off, even more so during the pandemic.

8

THE SPIRITUAL LIVES OF PRIESTS

T rying to measure one's spiritual state is a questionable endeavor. How does one measure or determine holiness? Relationship with God? Depth of the spiritual life? These intangibles remain beyond quantification. However, a study can measure external aspects of the spiritual life, spiritual practices, and a person's self-report on their spiritual state. We can use these to infer the presence or absence of a healthy spiritual life. But caution is always necessary. In the end, it is God who is the ultimate judge of such things.

We will look at the spiritual practices and self-report of the priests in the 2021 sample and compare those with the 2009 sample and, at times, with the 2004 sample.

THE SPIRITUAL PRACTICES OF PRIESTS ARE STRONG

The survey results in tables 8.1 and 8.2 indicate that the spiritual practices of priests in the United States, as a group, are strong, and by inference, their spiritual lives appear to be very healthy. In this 2021 survey, 90% report making an annual retreat; 95% strongly agree or agree that the Eucharist is the center of their lives; 95% strongly agree or agree to having a good relationship with God;

and 96% feel a sense of closeness to God. One priest wrote: "It's been a wonderful experience. Now I'm retired and gentle with myself as I age. I love God."

Table 8.1. Some spiritual practices of priests, 2021 and 2009 (%)

"I make an annual retreat"	Almost all the time	Usually	Sometimes	Rarely	Almost never
2009	62	18	11	6	3

"I make an annual retreat"	Yes	No
2021	90	10

"I have a regular spiritual director"	Yes	No
2021	52	48

"I receive the Sacrament of Penance"	At least weekly	Monthly	Every 3 months	Every 6 months	Yearly	Less than yearly
2009	4	25	28	19	12	11
2021	6	33	25	17	11	8

"I spent time in private prayer daily"	0–15 minutes	16–30 minutes	31–59 minutes	60 minutes or more
2009	19	30	31	20
2021	10	29	33	28

Table 8.2. Some aspects of Catholic priests' spirituality over three surveys

	Strongly agree (%)	Agree (%)	Unsure (%)	Disagree (%)	Strongly disagree (%)
"I pray all or most of the Liturgy of the Hours daily"					
2021	37	31	5	21	6
2009	30	28	10	24	9
"The Eucharist is the center of my life"					
2021	64	31	4	1	0
"I have a good relationship with God"					
2021	48	47	5	1	0
"I feel a sense of closeness to God"					
2021	53	43	4	1	0
2009	36	57	5	1	0
"I have a relationship with God (or Jesus) that is nourishing for me"					
2009	41	55	3	1	0
"I have a personal relationship with God (or Jesus) that is nourishing for me"					
2004	34	60	4	1	0
"I have a devotion to the Blessed Virgin Mary"					
2021	47	43	6	4	1
2009	25	48	16	9	2

Table 8.2. continued

	Strongly agree (%)	Agree (%)	Unsure (%)	Disagree (%)	Strongly disagree (%)
"Mary is an important part of my priestly life"					
2021	44	40	10	6	2
2009	27	45	16	10	2
"I believe God has called me to live a celibate life"					
2021	55	33	8	2	2
2009	33	45	14	6	2
"Despite its challenges, celibacy has been a grace for me personally"					
2021	37	45	12	4	2
2009	23	52	13	8	3
"Overall, celibacy has been a positive experience for me"					
2004	20	47	17	12	4

Moreover, 84–90% in the 2021 survey report having a good relationship with the Blessed Virgin Mary and consider her an important part of their priestly lives. One priest-respondent wrote:

- "In the wake of the [abuse] scandal, I lost my trust in the Church and still actively question whether/how much God is provident. Oddly enough, I still have great confidence in the care and love of Mary. My devotion to her has kept me knit together and close to her son."

Another wrote: "Jesus is my strength and Mama Mary is my inspiration to keep the flame of my vocation."

Interestingly, in 2021, 88% profess to believing God has called them to live a celibate life, and 82% say that "celibacy has been a grace for me personally." For the strong majority of priests, celibacy is viewed and experienced in a positive light. This does not mean that priests never struggle with their celibate calling. As some priests wrote:

- "I struggle with celibacy."

- "I am more and more convinced that mandatory celibacy is creating a problem in the priesthood."

- "I have been enjoying my priestly life. The one challenge I have been having is in the area of sexuality."

- "Yes, celibacy is a struggle, and I wish I could marry, but I offer it up and God gives me the grace."

Regarding the Sacrament of Penance and personal prayer, 81% go to Confession at least every six months, and 61% spend more than thirty minutes a day in private prayer. One could certainly debate how much time a priest ought to spend in daily private prayer, but to my mind, thirty minutes a day would be a minimum. In the residential treatment program for priests and religious in which I ministered, our spiritual department would begin the residents on a regimen of twenty minutes of private prayer a day and gradually increase it.

The good news is that the numbers are getting stronger. In 2009, 51% reported that they spent at least thirty minutes a day in private prayer; that number rose to 61% in 2021. Also, 68% in the 2021 survey strongly agreed or agreed that they prayed all or most of the Liturgy of the Hours daily. Given that deacons and priests have made a sacred promise in the presence of the bishop and the Church to pray the Liturgy of the Hours daily, this percentage is low. However, it is rising. In 2009, it was 58%.

These aforementioned elements are often thought to be integral parts of a priestly spirituality. Overall, given all the spiritual statistics in this survey, it seems that most priests have a strong devotional and relational spiritual life.

Perhaps what could use more emphasis is *formation* for personal prayer. In the seminary, such things are typically left to the private discussions of a seminarian and his spiritual director. I suggest that the priesthood might be well served to address as a community the subject of expectations and formation for prayer, including the practice and duration of daily private prayer and also the Liturgy of the Hours.

SPIRITUAL PRACTICES OF PRIESTS ARE INCREASING

There are unmistakable signs that the spiritual practices and self-reported spiritual relationships of priests are increasing. As just noted, more priests are praying the Liturgy of the Hours, up from 58% in 2009 to 68% in 2021, and more priests are praying at least thirty minutes a day, up from 51% in 2009 to 61% in 2021. Similarly, priests are going to Confession more often, from 76% receiving the sacrament at least every six months in 2009 to 81% in 2021.

In 2009, 36% of priests strongly agreed and 57% agreed that they "feel a sense of closeness to God." This compares with a larger 53% who strongly agreed in 2021 and 43% who agreed. Devotion to the Blessed Virgin Mary is increasing, from 73% in 2009 who strongly agreed or agreed to 90% in 2021. And a sense of being called by God to celibate living is likewise increasing, from 78% who strongly agreed or agreed in 2009 to 88% in 2021.

Perhaps their healthy spiritual practices help account for the resilience of priests in the wake of the COVID-19 pandemic and the sexual abuse crisis. One might speculate that these crises may have actually been catalysts for strengthening the spiritual lives of priests. When faced with personal and institutional stress, some priests will rely more heavily on their spiritual lives to sustain them. Well-established spiritual practices might be even more essential in such times.

YOUNGER PRIESTS HAVE A MORE TRADITIONAL SPIRITUALITY

It is commonly believed that younger priests today are more theologically traditional than older priests. The 2021 Survey of American Catholic Priests ($N = 1,036$) confirmed that perception with empirical findings.[1] In my study, there were clear signs that younger priests are more likely to engage in traditional spiritual practices as well, which complements their more theologically traditional outlook.

I separated the priests in my sample into six age groups, according to years of ordination (1–10, 11–20, 21–30, 31–40, 41–50, 51+ years ordained). The priests ordained 1–10 years reported higher rates of engaging in traditional spiritual practices. See table 8.3.

Table 8.3. Results of 2021 survey: Spiritual practices of newly ordained vs. older priests

	Years ordained	
	1–10 years (%)	40–50 years (%)
"I make an annual retreat"	97	86
"I have a regular spiritual director"	70	59
"I receive the Sacrament of Penance at least monthly"	71	23
"I pray privately each day 60 mins. or more"	31	24
"I believe God has called me to live a celibate life"	95	83
"I have a devotion to the Blessed Virgin Mary"	91	84
"I pray most or all of the Liturgy of the Hours daily"	79	59

Each of these differences is statistically significant (at least $p <$ .01) except for the amount of time spent in daily private prayer, that is, sixty minutes or more. More data are needed to confirm the statistical significance of that item.

But what is apparent from viewing the data is a slow curve showing an increasing support for these traditional practices from the older priests to the younger priests. For example, figure 8.1 shows younger priests frequenting the Sacrament of Penance more often than older priests.

In figure 8.1, 1 = less than yearly; 2 = yearly; 3 = every six months; 4 = every three months; 5 = monthly; 6 = at least weekly; and the Y-axis is the mean score of that group. The figure shows a gradual increase in frequency of reception of the Sacrament of Penance from older priests to younger priests.

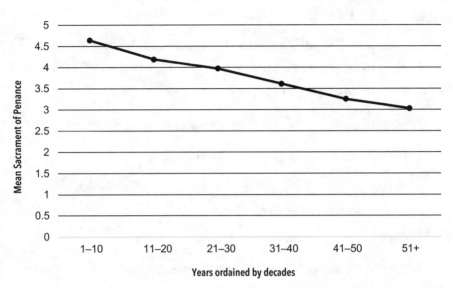

Figure 8.1. Frequenting the Sacrament of Penance by years ordained

We see the same gradual trend in whether the priest has a spiritual director or not. See figure 8.2.

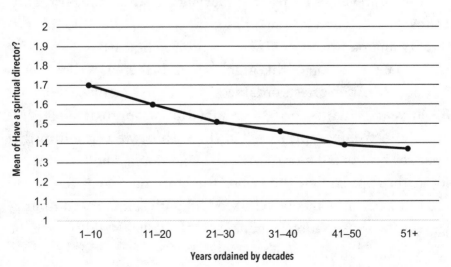

Figure 8.2. Having a spiritual director by years ordained
(1 = no, 2 = yes)

PRIESTS BECAME MORE TRADITIONAL AROUND 1990

After conducting a factor analysis and a Cronbach's alpha, eight spiritual variables loaded strongly on one component.[2] These eight items from the survey were:

- "I pray all or most of the Liturgy of the Hours daily."

- "I daily spend time in private prayer."

- "The Eucharist is the center of my life."

- "I have a good relationship with God."

- "I feel a sense of closeness to God."

- "Mary is an important part of my priestly life."

- "I have a devotion to the Blessed Virgin Mary."

- "I receive the Sacrament of Penance."

These items were then combined in a single variable, which I named Traditional Spirituality.

The mean values for this new variable, Traditional Spirituality, were computed and graphed to see if there is a difference in spirituality among priests of different ages. See figure 8.3.

Visual inspection of this graph suggests there is a slight jump in values between priests ordained 21–30 years and those ordained 31–40 years—that is, priests ordained after approximately 1990 and those ordained prior to that time. Thus, we can affirm that younger priests are more spiritually traditional, and we can also locate the approximate time when this shift may have occurred to around 1990. As someone who worked with seminary communities during those years, I can attest that the 1990s did seem to be a time when emphasis shifted toward a more traditional priestly spirituality. A review of the data supports that insight.

Figure 8.3. Traditional spirituality by years ordained

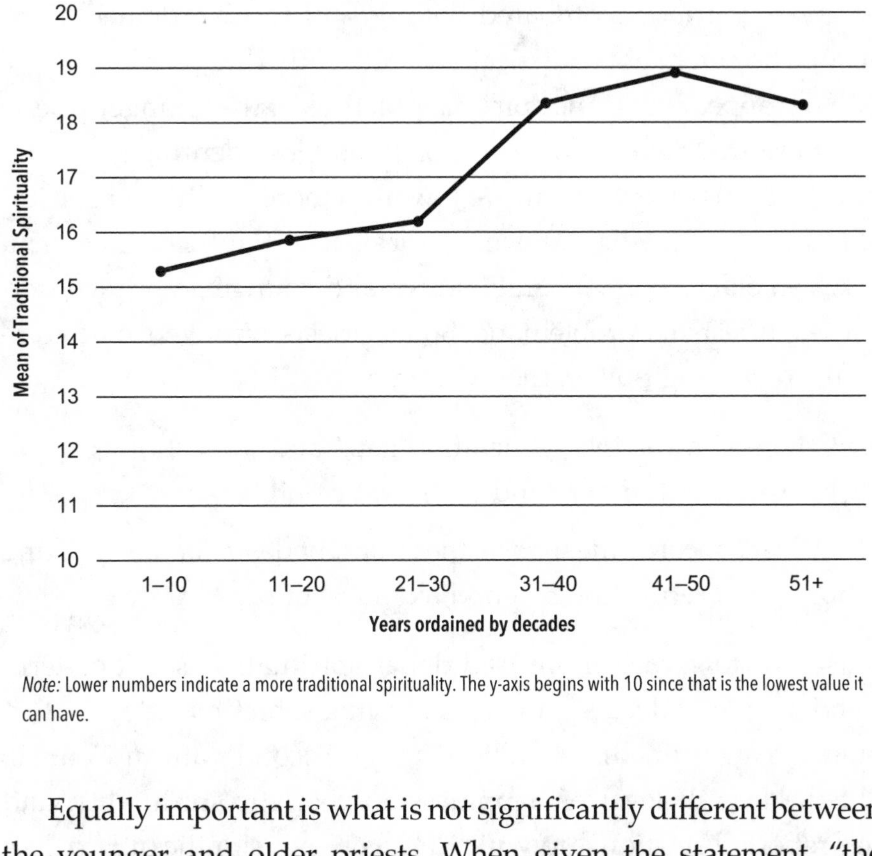

Note: Lower numbers indicate a more traditional spirituality. The y-axis begins with 10 since that is the lowest value it can have.

Equally important is what is not significantly different between the younger and older priests. When given the statement, "the Eucharist is the center of my life," 96% of the newly ordained strongly agreed or agreed, which was roughly comparable to 92% of those ordained 41–50 years. Similarly, 95% of the newly ordained strongly agreed or agreed with the statement, "I feel a sense of closeness to God," which was roughly equivalent to 94% of those ordained 41–50 years. Also, 93% of the newly ordained strongly agreed or agreed with the item "I have a good relationship with

God," compared with a similar 96% of priests ordained 41–50 years. Likewise, as noted previously, the younger priests self-reported a happiness level similar to older priests. Of the newly ordained, 92% strongly agreed or agreed with the statement, "Overall, I am happy as a priest," compared with 96% of those ordained 41–50 years. They were not statistically significantly different.

So it appears that the spiritual practices of the younger priests are more traditional. Some respondents who identified as older priests did not view this move toward a more traditional spirituality in a positive light. Several priests saw the theological split between older, more "liberal" priests and younger, more "conservative" priests as problematic. Some priests wrote specific comments regarding this on their surveys:

- "There is a distinct 'generation gap,' and a reaction to, or at least a lack of understanding of, Vatican II."

- "What concerns me most is the apparent desire of many young priests to return to 'the good old days' of pre-Vatican II."

This shift toward a more traditional spirituality is a long-term trend of several decades, likely beginning sometime after the turbulent years immediately following the Second Vatican Council. But the overall level of happiness, Eucharistic spirituality, and self-reported relationship with God were not significantly different when comparing younger and older priests. These all were encouragingly high for all ordination cohorts and remain a strength of the priesthood spanning many decades. As one priest wrote: "My faith anchors me. Hope, both for the world and for the Church, is harder to come by at times, but overall I trust God will bring us through."

9

PREDICTING VULNERABILITY IN A CRISIS

It is time to look more closely at the factors that enable a priest to weather a crisis with psychological and spiritual resiliency. In this study, we are examining the effects of two crises on the happiness and wellness of Catholic priests: the sexual abuse crisis in the Church and the COVID-19 pandemic. After running some statistical routines (a factor analysis and a Cronbach's alpha),[1] the data showed that the following survey items strongly coalesced into a single variable, which we will name Traumatized by the Crises:

- "The abuse crisis has negatively impacted my view of the priesthood."

- "The abuse crisis has negatively impacted my view of Church leadership."

- "The abuse crisis has negatively impacted my faith."

- "The COVID-19 pandemic has been traumatic for me personally."

- "The abuse crisis has negatively affected my emotional well-being."

- "I feel overwhelmed by the COVID-19 pandemic and need more support."

A New Variable: Traumatized by the Crises

This ability to combine the items related to the two crises is more understandable when we correlate the two items "The COVID-19 pandemic has been traumatic for me personally" and "The abuse crisis has negatively affected my emotional well-being." It turns out they are strongly correlated and thus are predictive of each other ($r = .45, p < .001$). Simply put, those who reported being traumatized by one crisis were more likely to report being traumatized by the other crisis. Those traumatized by the abuse crisis were more likely to be traumatized by the pandemic and vice versa.

This suggests that there are some priests, and likely all human beings, who are more susceptible to suffering personal trauma in the midst of a crisis, regardless of the type of crisis. Combining these six items related to the two crises into one variable, I ran statistical analyses to determine what some of these susceptibilities might be. What makes someone more vulnerable to being traumatized in a crisis?

After conducting Pearson's r correlations, I found that the following variables correlated significantly (at least at $p < .01$) with the combined variable Traumatized by the Crises. I set the cutoff at .20, and any correlations below that, although perhaps statistically significant, were not considered strong enough and thus not reported. The variables are listed in table 9.1 by highest correlation to least.

When these variables were entered into a multiple regression equation, the r squared was .27. This means that these variables account for about 27% of what makes a priest susceptible to being traumatized. While this is a good start, especially in social science research, it also suggests that more research is needed to determine the remaining variables.

Table 9.1. Variables correlated with the combined variable Traumatized by the Crises

	r
Loneliness	.44
Self-Esteem	-.42
Relationship with Bishop	-.33
ProQOL 5 Compassion Satisfaction	-.33
Childhood Trauma	.28
Traditional Spirituality	-.27
Priestly Fraternity	-.24
Sexual Conflicts	.23
Relationship with God	-.23
r^2	.27

Visual inspection of these variables yields some good information about what helps to protect a priest from being traumatized and, conversely, what makes him more vulnerable. As always, correlation does not automatically presume causation, so we will need to discuss these correlations in light of what we already know about priestly life and how trauma affects individuals.

MORE PRIESTLY FRATERNITY NEEDED

Some of the strongest predictors of vulnerability were related to priestly interpersonal connections such as found in the variables Loneliness and Priestly Fraternity. As we have seen earlier in this book, the issue of loneliness is a critical one for priests, and people in general. It is significantly predictive of one's vulnerability in a crisis. Fortunately, as we have noted, loneliness levels among priests appear to be much lower than those for the general population. However, when present, the negative effects of loneliness are strong. Now we can add that if a priest is isolated from other priests and people, he is more susceptible to suffering trauma in the midst of a crisis.

One unique and critical way that priests find connection is in priestly fraternity. The variable Priestly Fraternity is composed of three items: "I have close priest friends," "Priests in my diocese/religious order are supportive of each other," and "I attend priest gatherings in my diocese/order as often as I can." When performing a factor analysis, these three items loaded strongly on one component, and face validity suggests they measure priestly connections within a diocese/religious order.[2] Table 9.2 gives us the responses of the priests to these items for the 2021 and 2009 surveys.

Priests are not ordained into a private practice. They join a community of priests in a diocese or a religious order. This community carries some of the weight of a family and thus is important for a priest's health and wellness. In the midst of a crisis, the ability of priests to find support from brother priests is even more essential. The correlations noted in table 9.1 suggest that there is a connection between the mutual support within a presbyterate and the priest's ability to weather a crisis.

Table 9.2. Results of 2021, 2009 surveys: Priestly fraternity

"I have close priest friends"	Strongly agree (%)	Agree (%)	Unsure (%)	Disagree (%)	Strongly disagree (%)
2021	54	37	5	4	1
2009*	46	42	8	4	1

"Priests in my diocese/ religious order are supportive of each other"	Strongly agree (%)	Agree (%)	Unsure (%)	Disagree (%)	Strongly disagree (%)
2021	18	51	18	10	4
2009	10	59	18	10	3

"I belong to a priest support group"	Yes (%)	No (%)
2021	45	55

"I belong to a priest support group that meets regularly"	Yes (%)	No (%)
2009	37	63

*The question in the 2009 survey was slightly different: "I currently have close priest friends."

Visual inspection of the percentages in table 9.2 suggests that a strong majority of 2021 respondents, about 90%, have close priest friends, which is very good. It also appears that priestly fraternity has been stable throughout the recent decade and perhaps is improving somewhat. A few more priests are meeting in priest support groups, more strongly agree that priests are supportive of each other, and more have good priest friends. These slight increases in measures of priestly fraternity suggest modest improvement.

However, the overall percentages measuring priestly fraternity might be considered a bit low, for both 2009 and 2021. Only 69% strongly agree or agree that priests are supportive of each other. This was reflected in some of the written comments on respondents' surveys:

- "This diocese has an infestation of cliques among priests."
- "There seems to be a lot of division in the presbyterate. I sometimes wonder if anyone is listening to anyone who has a different opinion. This was a big surprise to me after ordination, as I didn't realize there was this much tension."
- "One of the greatest challenges I have experienced is the current lack of fraternity and shared support that seems to be part of our current presbyterate."
- "My individual experience is that in earlier years, bishops and priests worked together. . . . Today, there seems to be a palpable lack of unity."
- "I believe we must form intentional fraternities and friendships with fellow priests."

The social dynamics inside the Church often reflect dynamics in the wider society. The divide between "red" and "blue," so evident in secular politics and social divides in the United States, has become increasingly sharp and contentious. There is a similar divide in the Church as a whole and in the presbyterate as well. As some priest-respondents wrote:

- "One area of concern for me is the increasing division with the Church, especially in the United States. The celebration of the Eucharist has become a battleground for this division. It is increasingly challenging to connect with many of my brother priests."

- "The growing ideological and age divides among priests is very troubling."

Instead of decrying why priestly unity is fractured today, given the increasing polarization in society, one might wonder why it is as good as it is—and slightly improving. Nevertheless, priests acutely feel the pain of this division in the presbyterate. I have visited most dioceses in the United States in the past few decades and spoken with the priests. When they gather in small groups and discuss how they can improve priestly welfare, they *always* mention improving priestly unity and mutual support.

In these priestly gatherings, presbyterates typically recommend more priest support groups. They talk about the need for more priest gatherings, socially and liturgically. They raise the issue of the theological divide of young versus old, liberal versus conservative, pre-Vatican II versus post-Vatican II spiritualities. Priests recognize the need for all priests to work together in harmony while respecting individual differences. As one priest wrote, "I love my brother priests! And I love to foster the fraternity."

Because priestly unity is such an important factor for the health and happiness of our priests, as well as the efficacy of the Church's ministry, bishops ought to make priestly fraternity a priority. The bishop himself needs to be personally present at priest gatherings. It is always a huge draw for the priests when it is known that the bishop is coming to an event. Thankfully, in the priest convocations I have attended around the country, bishops universally have made it a priority to be personally present.

Seminaries and houses of formation ought to emphasize to future priests the value of attending priestly functions, for their own welfare as well as for the entire presbyterate. In both 2021 and in 2009, 80% of priests strongly agreed or agreed that they attend priest gatherings as often as they can. In fact, the number of those who strongly agreed increased from 28% to 40% from 2009 to 2021. So it appears that these gatherings are gaining in importance among priests. This is a salutary growth.

UNHEALED INNER WOUNDS INCREASE VULNERABILITY

There were three variables of past traumas and inner wounds that affected whether priests would be traumatized by the current crises. This only makes sense. If people have experienced trauma from their own unhealed inner wounds, the current crises will likely tap into these wounds and create even more psychic wounding. The trauma of today will feed off and deepen unhealed wounds from the past. These three variables were Self-Esteem ($r = -.42$), Childhood Trauma ($r = .28$), and Sexual Conflicts ($r = .23$).

As noted previously, the variable Self-Esteem is composed of two items on the survey:[3]

- "I have a good self-image."
- "I feel a sense of inner peace."

The variable Childhood Trauma is composed of these five items:[4]

- "I grew up in a dysfunctional family."
- "Growing up, I suffered from anxiety and/or depression."
- "As a child, I suffered from some trauma."
- "Growing up, I had a good relationship with my mother."
- "Growing up, I had a good relationship with my father."

And the variable Sexual Conflicts is composed of two items on the survey:[5]

- "I feel some conflict around my sexuality."
- "I know my sexual orientation and I am at peace with it."

Priests whose self-image was damaged and had a lack of inner peace were likely to be more traumatized by current crises. Similarly, those who explicitly suffered from childhood trauma were also likely to be more affected by the abuse crisis and the pandemic. The presence of self-reported inner sexual conflicts likewise contributed to a priest's vulnerability in a crisis. As one priest wrote on his survey: "The first few years [of priesthood] were difficult, clouded by depression due to my poor self-image. Two years of counseling made a big difference. Depression returned in the early 2000s due to the abuse crisis. . . . Then a profoundly moving spiritual experience changed my life. Joy in priestly ministry returned."

As someone who worked in a residential behavioral health center ministering to priests and religious for twenty years, I know that those who came for psychological healing were almost always suffering from wounds that originated in childhood. Many came for treatment after years of ministry, as the wounds of their childhood and other past traumas eventually came to the surface and needed healing. Their past woundedness resulted in their inability to cope with the stresses of the present.

Some priests who had been in psychotherapy wrote about how valuable it was for them:

- "My experience of priesthood has been generally good. I went through a period of time when I was unsure about my vocation. This coincides with my dealing with alcoholism. I spent five months in a treatment center—probably one of the best decisions I ever made."

- "During COVID, I've been seeing a counselor weekly for the past five months and it has made a tremendous difference in my personal mental, emotional, and spiritual well-being."

In my clinical experience at the treatment center, the vast majority of those who entered into treatment with an open heart and did their best experienced some amount of healing. Most made good progress. Many got much better. Some seemed to experience an almost miraculous depth and extent in their healing. Thankfully, in the 2009 survey, fully 46% of priest-respondents affirmed the statement, "During my priesthood, I have voluntarily sought out a counselor" and again in 2021, 39% agreed that "I have been in psychotherapy or counseling sometime during my priesthood." Thus, while unhealed traumas can negatively impact a priest's wellness, especially during a time of crisis, about 40% of priest-respondents have been in counseling since ordination and have thus overtly begun a healing journey.

RELATIONSHIP WITH BISHOP

The variable Relationship with Bishop is composed of two items: "I have a good relationship with my bishop" and "I support my bishop's leadership."[6] As noted previously, the relationship of a priest to his bishop is more than simply employer to employee. The relationship has strong theological and personal meaning for both parties. A solid relationship between a bishop and his priest is a strong predictor of priestly happiness ($r = .49, p < .001$).

Moreover, priests having a strong relationship with their bishop were less likely to have their trust in bishops shaken as a result of the crises. In the variable under consideration, Traumatized by the Crises, we again see that a strong relationship with the bishop can be a positive factor contributing to resilience in a crisis ($r = -.33, p < .001$).

SPIRITUALITY CONTRIBUTES TO RESILIENCE

It is important to note the contribution of a priest's spiritual life to resilience in a crisis. A strong relationship with God, as measured by the two items "I feel a sense of closeness to God" and "I have a good relationship with God," was statistically significant in its correlation with Traumatized by the Crises ($r = -.23, p < .001$). Similarly, Traditional Spirituality was likewise significantly correlated ($r = -.27, p < .001$).

So a solid spiritual connection to God combined with a strong, traditional spirituality was helpful in strengthening a priest's resilience in a crisis. Again, these traditional spiritual items included support for celibacy, daily private prayer and the Liturgy of the Hours, reception of the Sacrament of Penance, Eucharistic devotion, and a devotion to the Blessed Virgin Mary. Priests with a good relationship with the Lord plus daily prayer and a devotional life were more likely to weather the crises well and not be traumatized. One priest-respondent wrote: "Prayer is central—when my prayer is inauthentic, I get in my own head and cling to the world. When I am honest in prayer, it becomes freeing and healing."

In these days of reduced numbers of priests, the remaining priests are increasingly caught up in a flood of demands on their time. Many pastors have more than one parish. It is not unusual for a pastor to offer several Masses each weekend, in perhaps several locations. Some have a job in the bishop's chancery as well. Others combine those duties with special chaplaincies such as the police and fire chaplaincy, hospital and prison ministries, and the like. These increasing demands can easily squeeze out time for contemplation and prayer. This is a spiritually and psychologically dangerous dynamic, as this study statistically demonstrates.

Dioceses typically have an annual gathering of their priests. I mentioned earlier that it might be beneficial to devote one entire priestly convocation to fostering a priest's own spiritual life. If nothing else, such a convocation would send a strong message to its priests that they can and should daily take the time away from ministry to spend time with the Lord. In my own priestly life, I have come to realize that the effectiveness of my ministry is ultimately a result not of how much I work but of how much I love and allow the Lord to work through me.

YOUNG PRIESTS AND CHILDHOOD TRAUMA

When I compared younger with older priests, I found no significant differences on the variable Traumatized by the Crises. Thus, we can posit that younger and older priests were traumatized by the sexual abuse crisis and the pandemic approximately at the same rate. Years ordained was not a factor.

10

WHY ARE PRIESTS CRISIS RESILIENT?

Table 9.1 listed the variables in this study that most strongly predicted whether the current crises would be traumatic for priests, and thus conversely predicted crisis resilience. These variables indicate the factors that are important in protecting priests in a time of crisis and promoting their overall well-being. Again, they are:

- Loneliness ($r = .44$)
- Self-Esteem ($r = -.42$)
- Relationship with Bishop ($r = -.33$)
- ProQOL 5 Compassion Satisfaction ($r = -.33$)
- Childhood Trauma ($r = .28$)
- Traditional Spirituality ($r = -.27$)
- Priestly Fraternity ($r = -.24$)
- Sexual Conflicts ($r = .23$)
- Relationship with God ($r = -.23$)

Let us now look at how priests as a group are doing with regard to each of these important variables. This might also help us understand the very positive findings of priestly resilience that surfaced in this study. As noted, the results of the ProQOL 5 test indicate that Burnout rates in priesthood are low; priests score high on Compassion Satisfaction, indicating strong satisfaction with their ministries; and they score low on Secondary Trauma, suggesting they are not acutely traumatized by the recent crises.

The BSI-18 results indicated that rates of depression among priests rose from 7.5% before the pandemic to 14.5% during the pandemic. Their rate of anxiety rose from 6.4% to 9.3%. As one priest-respondent wrote, "The pandemic has been extremely taxing on me. . . . I certainly feel a lot of fear and anxiety about it." While this significant increase in anxiety and depression should be cause for concern, the US Census Bureau numbers reported a much higher (fourfold) rise in depression and anxiety for the general population.

So the test findings suggest that priests as a group are more resilient than the general population in a crisis. This is not to say that the pandemic and the sexual abuse crisis were not stressful and had no impact. Fully 19% strongly agreed or agreed that the "abuse crisis has negatively affected my emotional well-being." And 31% strongly agreed or agreed that "the COVID-19 pandemic has been traumatic for me personally." However, the respondents' level of traumatization did not typically rise to clinical levels, and their basic mental health, wellness, and happiness remained relatively stable.

Moreover, priestly happiness rates seem to be consistently rising over several decades. In my three studies in response to the statement, "Overall, I am happy as a priest," those who strongly agreed or agreed rose from 90% in 2004, to 92% in 2009, to 94% in 2021.

When looking at such positive results, some will be skeptical. However, investigating the results more deeply, we see solid indications why they are likely to be accurate. When we look at individual variables that affect resilience in a crisis, we can see some of the strengths of priests and why these findings are most likely to be true. The following are the nine variables that surfaced as predicting resilience in a crisis and a snapshot of how priests are currently doing with each variable based upon our 2021 survey results.

Loneliness

Self-reported loneliness was a strong variable in predicting vulnerability in a crisis. Compared with the general population, priesthood loneliness rates were much lower. When respondents were given the statement, "I suffer from loneliness," only 21% strongly agreed or agreed. Similarly, in response to the BSI-18 item asking about loneliness, only 24% of priests indicated they felt lonely "moderately," "quite a bit," or "extremely," as opposed to 76% who said "not at all" or "a little bit." This appears to be considerably lower than the general population. As previously noted, the 2018 Cigna study reported an "epidemic of loneliness" in which 54% of Americans confessed to being lonely.

Priests report being strongly connected to others. As previously noted, 91% of the respondents strongly agreed or agreed with the statement, "I have close priest friends," and 96% strongly agreed or agreed with the item "I have good lay friends." One priest wrote on his survey: "I recently lost my father due to COVID and have been sustained by faith and the goodness of many people, most of whom are my priest friends from all over the world. This experience moves me greatly. I see the value of being a priest and the value of fraternity in the priesthood during good and bad times."

Self-Esteem

The variable Self-Esteem was almost equally predictive as the variable Loneliness of vulnerability in a crisis. The self-reported self-esteem of our priests was high. In response to one of the two items that made up this composite variable, "I feel a sense of inner peace," 89% strongly agreed or agreed. Similarly, in response to the second item in this composite variable, "I have a good self-image," 86% strongly agreed or agreed. One might conclude that about 87% of priests have a good internal sense of self and inner peace. This, too, is a strong finding and critical in weathering a crisis.

In comparison, one article in *Psychology Today* suggested that 85% of people around the world suffer from poor self-esteem.[1] While it is likely that these numbers are not completely comparable to the measures in this study, it seems clear that priestly self-esteem rates are probably higher than those of the general population.

Relationship with Bishop

A priest's relationship with his bishop is a solid predictor of resilience in a crisis. In response to the item "I have a good relationship with my bishop," 73% strongly agreed or agreed, and 80% strongly agreed or agreed with the statement, "I support my bishop's leadership."

This survey found that 55% of priests say that the abuse crisis has negatively affected their view of Church leadership. This is high! But it seems that priests distinguish between bishops as a whole and their own bishop. While priests' trust in bishops declined significantly because of the abuse crisis, their support for their own bishops remained strong, particularly in comparison with the relationship of laypeople with their secular bosses.

The positive connection between most priests and their bishops is yet another strength for the presbyterate and a support for resilience in a crisis.

ProQOL 5 Compassion Satisfaction

One of the strongest factors for resilience is liking and finding nourishment in one's priestly ministry. This is identified by the ProQOL 5 Compassion Satisfaction scale. It certainly makes sense that those who are happy with their own priestly ministry are more likely to weather a crisis well. Indeed, in the midst of these crises, priests who were committed to their ministry and found it personally fulfilling realized the importance of their work. Many priests witnessed their people suffering greatly in the sexual abuse crisis as well as in the pandemic and did what they could to minister to their hurting congregations.

For example, many priests found creative ways to connect and minister to their parishioners during the pandemic. Many livestreamed the Mass; others heard Confessions outside the church from parishioners in their cars; others prayed with and counseled people over the phone. I was encouraged and edified by what so many of my brother priests did to help their people cope with the pandemic. Rather than focusing on their own suffering, many sought first to relieve the suffering of others.

Research consistently shows that those who engage in helping others in the midst of a crisis or trauma are more likely themselves to cope well. For example, the research study of Nancy Sin and her colleagues in the midst of the pandemic found that "prosocial activities were associated with higher positive affect and greater social satisfaction on days when they occurred. Providing COVID-19-related support further predicted lower same-day negative affect."[2] Thus, those who were occupied with helping others during the pandemic were more likely to report feeling happy and satisfied. This helps us understand why priests were reporting higher levels of happiness and satisfaction than the general population during these crises.

The numbers in this survey bear out this finding. As we saw in table 3.2, 92% of priests say they very often or often "like my work as a [priest]"; 88% very often or often feel satisfied with their work; and 93% are happy to have chosen to be a priest.

This is in striking comparison with the Conference Board's 2020 findings from 5,000 US households. Only 57% of the general population reports being satisfied overall with their jobs. This is a decrease from 61% in 1987, although it is an increase from a low 43% in 2010.[3] These high job satisfaction rates of the clergy are supported by the findings of the General Social Survey of the National Opinion Research Center (NORC). In a 2006 survey of 27,000 Americans, clergy had the highest job satisfaction and happiness of any occupation: 87% reported being very satisfied.[4]

One of the greatest strengths of priesthood is the consistent and strong satisfaction with priestly ministry. It is rare to hear of a priest who does not like ministering to the people.

Childhood Trauma

A consistent finding in this study is the deleterious effects of childhood dysfunction and trauma, when not healed. As previously noted, the combined variable Childhood Trauma comprises five items:

- "I grew up in a dysfunctional family."
- "Growing up, I suffered from anxiety and/or depression."
- "As a child, I suffered from some trauma."
- "Growing up, I had a good relationship with my mother."

- "Growing up, I had a good relationship with my father."

We will look at these items individually and see how priests responded in the survey. In response to the item "I grew up in a dysfunctional family," 19% strongly agreed or agreed. In response to the item "As a child, I suffered from some trauma," 22% strongly agreed or agreed. For the statement, "Growing up, I had a good relationship with my mother," 94% strongly agreed or agreed, and for "Growing up, I had a good relationship with my father," 80% strongly agreed or agreed. In response to the item "Growing up, I suffered from anxiety and/or depression," 20% strongly agreed or agreed.

Are these numbers good or bad? Objectively speaking, having 20% of the presbyterate growing up in dysfunctional families is not a positive finding. Nevertheless, even greater percentages of Americans report growing up with at least one Adverse Childhood Experience (ACE). These experiences include sexual, physical, or psychological abuse; living in a household with substance abusers; having mentally ill or suicidal family members; having imprisoned family members; and witnessing violent acts against the mother.

In a study by V. J. Felitti and colleagues, more than 50% of the 9,000+ adults in the survey said they experienced at least one ACE. Other studies report even higher numbers.[5] In 2019, a CDC study of 144,000 adults found that 61% of Americans reported at least one ACE in childhood and 16% had four or more.[6] So it appears to be a relatively positive finding that the large majority of priests reported a childhood that was largely free of trauma and dysfunction and was characterized by good relationships with both parents, especially with mothers. However, I remain concerned that 20% of priests reported such a background and its possible deleterious effects.

Traditional Spirituality

The composite variable Traditional Spirituality comprises eight survey items:

- "I pray all or most of the Liturgy of the Hours daily."

- "I spend time in private prayer daily."

- "The Eucharist is the center of my life."

- "I have a good relationship with God."

- "I feel a sense of closeness to God."

- "Mary is an important part of my priestly life."

- "I have a devotion to the Blessed Virgin Mary."

- "I receive the Sacrament of Penance."

Looking at the responses of the priests, there is obviously a strong commitment by the majority to living a spiritual life:

- 61% of priests say that they pray privately more than thirty minutes a day.

- 64% receive the Sacrament of Penance at least every three months (92% profess receiving this sacrament at least yearly).

- 95% strongly agree or agree that "the Eucharist is the center of my life."

- 95% strongly agree or agree that they have a good relationship with God and that they feel a sense of closeness to God.

- 90% strongly agree or agree that they have a devotion to the Blessed Virgin Mary.

- 83% strongly agree or agree that "Mary is an important part of my priestly life."

In addition, the strong majority are committed to living a celibate life: 88% strongly agree or agree that God has called them to live a celibate life, and 82% strongly agree or agree that "celibacy has been a grace for me personally." This is quite remarkable, and it suggests that the majority of priests embrace the practice and spirituality of priestly celibacy.

It seems clear that one of the great strengths of the priesthood in the United States is the priests' commitment to nurturing their spiritual lives using traditional spiritual practices: prayer, the Sacrament of Penance, the Eucharist, devotion to Mary, and fostering a strong relationship with God. Also, they feel called to live a celibate life and find it has been a grace for them. This solid spiritual life is a strength in a time of crisis.

However, we should not overlook these findings:

- About one-third of priests are praying thirty minutes or fewer a day.

- 8% do not go to Confession even yearly.

- 5% do not feel they have a good relationship with God.

- 5% do not have a strong Eucharistic spirituality.

Using SPSS software to make a crosstabs calculation, I looked at some of these individuals. It is notable that of those priests who prayed more than thirty minutes per day and went to Confession at least monthly, 99% said they were happy as priests. While we need to be careful in assigning cause and effect, we can certainly say that happy priests are more likely to engage in the traditional spiritual practices of a priest.

Priestly Fraternity

The unity of the Church in general, and the unity of priesthood in particular, is an important theological concept. Jesus prayed that "they may all be one" (Jn 17:21). As noted previously, it is a bit disturbing that 29% of priests indicated that "the abuse crisis has negatively impacted my view of the priesthood" and that only 69% of priests believe that priests are supportive of each other in their dioceses.

We have seen how important priestly fraternity is for resilience in a crisis and noted that in priestly gatherings priests *always* mention the need for more such gatherings and increased mutual support. It may be that priestly unity is much stronger than that of the general population, although this is little consolation in a time of crisis.

One indicator of priestly fraternity is solid: 91% of priests say they have close relationships with other priests. And the percentage of priests who belong to a priest support group has risen from 37% in 2009 to 45% in 2021. The ability of priests to weather a crisis is firmly connected to the solidarity of the presbyterate. The ones who know and experience this are the priests themselves. In a time when the nation is wracked by conflicts and divisions, priestly unity is itself threatened and, at the same time, even more essential.

Sexual Conflicts

The variable Sexual Conflicts is composed of two items on the survey: "I feel some conflict around my sexuality" and "I know my sexual orientation and I am at peace with it." The correlation between resilience in a crisis and one's sexual conflicts was significant $r = .23$ ($p < .001$). Being at peace with one's inner self, including one's sexuality, is a positive support for weathering external crises.

Many years ago, the need to understand and integrate one's sexuality in a healthy way was not considered essential for a celibate priest. The findings in this survey reaffirm the importance for all people, including celibate priests, of integrating one's sexuality in a healthy and holy way, as appropriate for one's vocational calling. Fortunately, a strong 94% of priest-respondents say that they are at peace with their sexuality and a lesser 22% say they experience some conflict around their sexuality. So the great majority of priests today feel they are coping in a positive way with their sexuality.

One would expect that this variable would be related to Childhood Trauma and, in fact, the correlation between the two variables is statistically significant ($p < .001$), although it was a modest $r = .28$. So it is likely that being at peace with one's sexuality is related to the presence or absence of childhood trauma and one's early developmental experiences, but there is more to it as well.

Learning to manage one's sexuality as an adult in a ministerial context is a challenge for the priest of today, especially with the plethora of non-Christian images that bombard people's senses in our culture on a daily basis. I recently spoke with a bishop who was saddened to learn of two young priests in his diocese leaving the priesthood for a coupled relationship. It was difficult for the presbyterate as well.

The work of learning to be fully alive as an authentic celibate priest is never finished. Each phase of life brings new challenges. Centuries of accumulated wisdom suggest that the ability to live an authentic celibate life is closely connected with all the other variables in this study, including the depth of one's spiritual life and the presence of life-giving relationships with other priests, God, and oneself.

Relationship with God

The final variable that factors into a priest's resilience in a crisis is Relationship with God. This combined variable is composed of two survey items: "I have a good relationship with God" and "I feel a sense of closeness to God." It is difficult to imagine a priest spiritually and psychologically prospering in priesthood without such a relationship. This study confirms its importance for crisis resilience among priests.

Crises often raise theological questions and doubts in the minds of the faithful: how could God allow such a terrible thing to happen? One's theological worldview can be shaken by trauma and tragedy. So, too, for a priest. If his own faith and relationship with God are weak, not only will he likely have problems helping others, but he may be thrown into a personal spiritual crisis. Responses to the 2021 survey showed that 8% of priests strongly agreed or agreed with the statement, "The abuse crisis has negatively impacted my faith." While the percentage is small, it is certainly not insignificant.

The good news is that in all three surveys (2004, 2009, and 2021), 93–96% of priests strongly agreed or agreed to having a good relationship with God. A strong relationship with God, which is almost unanimously felt by priests, is a bedrock for the health and resilience of priests.

A GENERATION OF SURVIVORS

The overall strong results in these nine categories give a sense of why priests are so resilient and continue to report good psychological and spiritual health, despite the intense crises they have had to endure. But it makes perfect sense: a priest who has a solid sense of self-esteem, who experienced a childhood relatively free of trauma, who enjoys good relationships with other priests, God, and his bishop, who has a strong spiritual life, and who finds satisfaction in his priestly ministry is likely to weather a crisis much more easily than a priest lacking or weak in any of these areas. Fortunately, the numbers suggest that priests in the United States, as a group, are strong in all these variables. A visual inspection of the percentages in each of these categories suggests that 75–90% of priests in the sample generally fall into the category of crisis resilient. As one priest wrote on his survey, "I think that our generation of priests have become 'survivors.'"

11

A NEW MEGA VARIABLE: PRIEST WELLNESS

W e have discussed how the following variables most strongly predicted whether the two crises addressed in the 2021 study affected priests:

- Loneliness ($r = .44$)

- Self-Esteem ($r = -.42$)

- Relationship with Bishop ($r = -.33$)

- ProQOL 5 Compassion Satisfaction ($r = -.33$)

- Childhood Trauma ($r = .28$)

- Traditional Spirituality ($r = -.27$)

- Priestly Fraternity ($r = -.24$)

- Sexual Conflicts ($r = .23$)

- Relationship with God ($r = -.23$)

These are essentially the same variables that most strongly predicted whether a priest is happy, whether he will be depressed or burned out, and the state of his overall mental health.[1] These combined results are compiled in table 11.1 (all reported correlations are statistically significant, $p < .001$).

Table 11.1. Four major variables*

	Traumatized by the crises	BSI-18 GSI (mental health)	Priestly happiness	ProQOL 5 burnout
Loneliness	.44	-.66	-.50	-.54
Self-esteem	-.42	.53	.66	.63
Relationship with bishop	-.33	.26	.49	.36
ProQOL 5				
Compassion satisfaction	-.33	.43	.62	.66
Childhood trauma	.28	-.37	-.32	-.32
Traditional spirituality	-.27	.23	.44	.28
Priestly fraternity	-.24	.29	.45	.31
Sexual conflicts	.23	-.25	-.25	-.21
Relationship with God	-.23	.31	.50	.41
$r^2 =$	.27	.51	.63	.58

*The sign value (+ or -) may be changed in different places in this manuscript for statistical reasons, e.g., in order to properly combine the individual items into a larger combined variable.

When these variables were entered into a multiple regression equation for each of the four composite variables, they predicted a significant percentage of each (Traumatized by the Crises, $r^2 = .27$; BSI-18 GSI, $r^2 = .51$; Priestly Happiness, $r^2 = .63$; ProQOL 5 Burnout, $r^2 = .58$).[2] Thus, we are able to predict:

- 27% of whether a crisis will be traumatic for a priest,
- 51% of a priest's overall mental health,
- 63% of what makes a priest happy, and

- 58% of what leads to burnout.

In social science research, these are solid findings. Moreover, since these same variables predict all four of these major constructs (resilience in crisis, mental health, happiness, and burnout), they are even more important for their impact on the life of a priest.

Variables such as these are often interrelated; that is, they exhibit multicollinearity. They are all intertwined in a mutual interaction. Happy priests are less likely to suffer from depression or anxiety, less likely to be burned out, and less likely to be traumatized in a crisis. Similarly, priests who suffer from depression or anxiety are more likely to be burned out, vulnerable to being traumatized in a crisis, and less likely to be happy in their lives and ministries. Traumatized priests are less likely to be happy and more likely to suffer from depression or anxiety and be burned out. Burned-out priests are more likely to suffer from anxiety or depression, be unhappy in priesthood, and are more susceptible to being traumatized in a crisis. All of these variables mutually interact and affect each other in the life of a priest.

A NEW OVERARCHING CONCEPT: PRIESTLY WELLNESS

Calculating the Pearson's r correlation for the four variables (Priestly Happiness, Burnout, Mental Health, Traumatized by the Crises) indicates that these four major constructs are indeed highly correlated. The correlations for all of the pairs ranged from .46 to .65. After doing a factor analysis and then a Cronbach's alpha (.71), we see that these variables definitely lend themselves to being combined into one overarching mega variable. This new variable might be named Priestly Wellness, Happiness, and Resilience—or perhaps simply Priestly Wellness.

Thus, the wellness, happiness, and resilience of our priests, and likely all people, might be thought of as one mega concept. This new variable measures the overall psychological and spiritual health of a person, and in this case, a priest. Once again, calculating correlations and conducting a regression analysis on this new overarching variable, Priestly Wellness, yielded strong statistical results. See table 11.2.

Table 11.2. Correlations of nine variables with Priestly Wellness

	Priestly Wellness (r)
Loneliness	-.68
Self-Esteem	.65
ProQOL 5 Compassion Satisfaction	.57
Relationship with God	.40
Childhood Trauma	-.40
Relationship with Bishop	.38
Priestly Fraternity	.36
Traditional Spirituality	.32
Sexual Conflicts	-.28
$r^2 =$	.64*

*All are statistically significant, p < .001.

Regressing all of these variables on Priestly Wellness yielded a high $r^2 = .64$ (p < .001). So we can predict 64% of what makes a priest psychologically and spiritually well! This is a very strong finding.

It was exciting to witness the statistical emergence of this mega concept. Frankly, it makes sense. A person is not split into subcategories. We look at different aspects of a person to help understand the whole individual better. But each of us is one unified person. We are body, psyche, and spirit all combined into one. Each aspect interpenetrates and informs the others. What happens to us on one level affects the others. The emergence of this one mega variable is a statistical demonstration of this truth. Moreover, it can help focus more sharply the goals of a program of formation and ongoing growth for a priest—and likely for anyone.

When helping priests understand important personal strengths and weaknesses, we might look at these variables and ask how they fare in these areas. Is their house "built on rock," or is it "built on sand"? (Mt 7:24–27). When a crisis comes along, does the wind destroy the house, or is it able to weather the storm? The resilience of most of our priests became apparent upon review of how they are currently doing with these variables. Their house is built solidly upon rock.

12

LISTENING TO THE MANY HAPPY PRIESTS

It was a privilege and an encouragement to read the hundreds of comments that priest-respondents voluntarily wrote at the end of their completed surveys. There were certainly some who were upset, angry, and disillusioned. But they were in the small minority. The overwhelming tone of the vast majority of comments was positive; the priests expressed gratitude and often witnessed to the sanctity of their own lives. I share some of these so that you, too, may hear the joy in their hearts and glimpse the satisfaction of their priestly lives:

- "Overall priesthood has been terrific!"
- "I have a strong feeling of joy as a priest of this diocese."
- "Priesthood is a special gift from God."
- "I love being a priest and have never regretted it."
- "I love it. God is good!"
- "When I think about the priesthood, my primary feeling is one of gratitude. I never imagined it would be this wonderful a life."
- "I love my vocation."
- "I find my life as a priest very rewarding and fulfilling."

- "I am a happy priest and a happy pastor."
- "I love my life and my priesthood."
- "Being a priest is a beautiful gift from God."
- "Blessed be God. I love what I am doing."
- "I cannot imagine not being a priest!"
- "I love being a priest and I can't imagine a more fulfilling life."
- "I thank God every day for my priesthood."
- "My time as a priest has been full and rich."
- "Priesthood has been more of a gift than I could have ever imagined."
- "I absolutely love my priesthood. Unworthy as I feel, I thank God for this calling, and try to respond daily to the best of my ability."
- "I would do it all again."

TROUBLING TRENDS IN AMERICA

In interpreting the data in this survey, I often compared the results of priest-respondents to those of the general population in similar surveys. This is important. Statistics by themselves can be variously interpreted based upon the biases of the researcher, something that happens especially when making inferences about the lives of Catholic priests. So, it is essential to compare the numbers that surface in a research study with something. For example, if a certain percentage of priests say that they suffer from loneliness, is that good or bad? One way to make such judgments is by comparing them with the general population, which I often did.

But in the process of this frequent comparison, I noted one disturbing trend. While the lives of priests, as measured in the past few decades, appear to be getting better, the lives of the rest of the population appear to be getting worse—dramatically worse.

Priesthood in the United States is likely benefiting from the increased emphasis on screening and formation, particularly in human formation. The John Jay study, accomplished in the wake of the 2002 sexual abuse crisis, found that human formation programs were effective in reducing rates of subsequent abuse by priests.[1] Screening and human formation work!

Moreover, the elements of a happy and well life are largely encapsulated in a priestly life well lived. Such elements typically include good relationships, a solid self-esteem, meaningful work, a life dedicated to helping others, and a strong spirituality. These are essential elements in a priest's life and help to explain why priests have been and remain among the happiest of Americans. Such a statement is itself countercultural, but the statistical facts are clear.

However, rates of depression and anxiety within the general population have quadrupled in the midst of the pandemic. Dissatisfaction with work is rising; more than half of US workers are unhappy with their jobs.[2] Loneliness among Americans is at epidemic levels. Suicide rates have increased by 35% in the United States from 1999 to 2018, according to the CDC.[3] Membership in houses of worship in the United States dropped from about 70% in 2000 to 47% in 2020 with a concomitant rise in unaffiliated individuals and atheism/agnosticism.[4] Anger, division, and violence seem to be dramatically on the rise. Not so long ago, it would have been unthinkable that someone would walk into a school or a crowded mall and start shooting innocent people. Yet such has become commonplace. A large 72% of Americans think the country is headed in the wrong direction.[5]

The lessons in this research point a way out of our psychological and spiritual decline as Americans. While the life of a priest has unique aspects, the basic dynamics of what makes a priest healthy and happy can be applied to the population at large. Any mental health professional would agree that solid human relationships, good self-esteem, inner healing from childhood traumas, and finding satisfaction in one's work are critical for the health and welfare of any person. This study adds to those insights. A relationship with God, a connection with a believing community, work that serves others, and traditional spiritual practices such as daily private prayer are also important for nurturing the whole person.

As a result of their daily living of these realities, the wellness of our priests in the United States, as a whole, is strong and getting stronger. At the same time, as these values appear to be declining in significant parts of the country, our populace may experience increasing psychological and spiritual problems.

I have no doubt that these reflections will give rise to some critical responses. All I can say is that the insights in this book are where the data have led me. My request is that people debate these ideas from a stance of solid data, as done in this book, rather than from personal conjecture or anecdotal information. If you disagree, what data do you have to support your statement? I welcome such a debate.

APPENDIX 1

THE 2021 SURVEY OF PRIESTS

When you help people, you have direct contact in their lives. As you may have found, your compassion for those you help can affect you in positive and negative ways. Below are some questions about your experiences, both positive and negative, as a [helper/priest]. Consider each of the following questions about yourself and your current work situation. Select the number that honestly reflects how frequently you experienced these things during the *last thirty days*.

1. Never   2. Rarely   3. Sometimes   4. Often   5. Very Often

_____ 1. I am happy.

_____ 2. I am preoccupied with more than one person I help.

_____ 3. I get satisfaction from being able to help others.

_____ 4. I feel connected to others.

_____ 5. I jump or am startled by unexpected sounds.

_____ 6. I feel invigorated after working with those I help.

_____ 7. I find it difficult to separate my personal life from my life as a [helper/priest].

_____ 8. I am not as productive at work because I am losing sleep over traumatic experiences of a person I help.

_____ 9. I think I might have been affected by the traumatic stress of those I help.

_____ 10. I feel trapped by my job as a [helper/priest].

_____ 11. Because of my helping, I have felt "on edge" about various things.

_____ 12. I like my work as a [helper/priest].

_____ 13. I feel depressed because of the traumatic experiences of the people I help.

_____ 14. I feel as though I am experiencing the trauma of someone I have helped.

_____ 15. I have beliefs that sustain me.

_____ 16. I am pleased with how I am able to keep up with helping techniques and protocols.

_____ 17. I am the person I always wanted to be.

_____ 18. My work makes me feel satisfied.

_____ 19. I feel worn out because of my work as a [helper/priest].

_____ 20. I have happy thoughts and feelings about those I help and how I could help them.

_____ 21. I feel overwhelmed because my [case/work] load seems endless.

_____ 22. I believe I can make a difference through my work.

_____ 23. I avoid certain activities or situations because they remind me of frightening experiences of the people I help.

_____ 24. I am proud of what I can do to help.

_____ 25. As a result of helping, I have intrusive, frightening thoughts.

_____ 26. I feel "bogged down" by the system.

_____ 27. I have thoughts that I am a "success" as a [helper/priest].

_____ 28. I can't recall important parts of my work with trauma victims.

_____ 29. I am a very caring person.

_____ 30. I am happy that I chose to do this work.

Age _____ Years Ordained _____

What country were you born in? _____

What is your current ministry? (*Circle all that apply.*)

   Parish / Hospital Chaplain / Chancery / Retired / Other

Check or circle the appropriate response:

I am a:

☐ religious priest ☐ diocesan priest

I have a regular spiritual director:

☐ yes ☐ no

I belong to a priest support group:

□ yes □ no

I make an annual retreat:

□ yes □ no

I like to be the center of attention:

□ yes □ no

I daily spend time in private prayer:

□ 0–15 mins. □ 16–30 mins. □ 31–59 mins. □ 60 mins. or more

I have been in psychotherapy or counseling sometime during my priesthood:

□ yes □ no

I receive the Sacrament of Penance:

□ at least weekly   □ monthly   □ every 3 mos.   □ every 6 mos.
□ yearly   □ less than yearly

**SA = strongly agree   A = agree   U = unsure   D = disagree
SD = strongly disagree**

1. I have close priest friends.	SA	A	U	D
2. I have good lay friends.	SA	A	U	D
3. The Eucharist is the center of my life.	SA	A	U	D
4. My morale as a priest is good.	SA	A	U	D
5. I am thinking of leaving the priesthood.	SA	A	U	D
6. I have a good relationship with God.	SA	A	U	D

7. Overall, I am happy as a priest.	SA	A	U	D
8. If I had to do it all over again, I would still become a priest.	SA	A	U	D
9. The abuse crisis has negatively impacted my view of the priesthood.	SA	A	U	D
10. The abuse crisis has negatively impacted my view of Church leadership.	SA	A	U	D
14. I actively encourage men to become priests.	SA	A	U	D
15. The COVID-19 pandemic has been traumatic for me personally.	SA	A	U	D
16. The abuse crisis has negatively affected my emotional well-being.	SA	A	U	D
17. I feel overwhelmed by the COVID-19 pandemic and need more support.	SA	A	U	D
18. I support my bishop's leadership.	SA	A	U	D

Read each statement carefully and circle the number of the response that best describes how much that problem has distressed or bothered you during the past seven days, including today. Circle only one number for each problem (0 1 2 3 4).

0 = Not at all   1 = A little bit   2 = Moderately   3 = Quite a bit   4= Extremely

How much were you distressed by:

1. Faintness or dizziness	0	1	2	3	4
2. Feeling no interest in things	0	1	2	3	4
3. Nervousness or shakiness inside	0	1	2	3	4
4. Pains in heart or chest	0	1	2	3	4
5. Feeling lonely	0	1	2	3	4

0 = Not at all   1 = A little bit   2 = Moderately   3 = Quite a bit   4 = Extremely

	0	1	2	3	4
6. Feeling tense or keyed up	0	1	2	3	4
7. Nausea or upset stomach	0	1	2	3	4
8. Feeling blue	0	1	2	3	4
9. Suddenly scared for no reason	0	1	2	3	4
10. Trouble getting your breath	0	1	2	3	4
11. Feelings of worthlessness	0	1	2	3	4
12. Spells of terror or panic	0	1	2	3	4
13. Numbness or tingling in parts of your body	0	1	2	3	4
14. Feeling hopeless about the future	0	1	2	3	4
15. Feeling so restless you couldn't sit still	0	1	2	3	4
16. Feeling weak in parts of your body	0	1	2	3	4
17. Thoughts of ending your life	0	1	2	3	4
18. Feeling fearful	0	1	2	3	4

SA = strongly agree   A = agree   U = unsure   D = disagree
SD = strongly disagree

1. I have a devotion to the Blessed Virgin Mary.	SA	A	U	D	SD
2. I believe God has called me to live a celibate life.	SA	A	U	D	SD
3. I feel a sense of closeness to God.	SA	A	U	D	SD
4. Growing up, I had a good relationship with my mother.	SA	A	U	D	SD
5. Growing up, I had a good relationship with my father.	SA	A	U	D	SD
6. I feel some conflict around my sexuality.	SA	A	U	D	SD
7. I know my sexual orientation and I am at peace with it.	SA	A	U	D	SD
8. I grew up in a dysfunctional family.	SA	A	U	D	SD
9. I exercise on a regular basis.	SA	A	U	D	SD
10. Despite its challenges, celibacy has been a grace for me personally.	SA	A	U	D	SD
11. Growing up, I suffered from anxiety and/or depression.	SA	A	U	D	SD
12. I pray most or all of the Liturgy of the Hours daily.	SA	A	U	D	SD
13. I have a good self-image.	SA	A	U	D	SD
14. I suffer from loneliness.	SA	A	U	D	SD
15. I attend priest gatherings in my diocese/order as often as I can.	SA	A	U	D	SD
16. As a child, I suffered from some trauma.	SA	A	U	D	SD
17. Mary is an important part of my priestly life.	SA	A	U	D	SD
18. Priests in my diocese/religious order are supportive of each other.	SA	A	U	D	SD
19. I take a day off each week.	SA	A	U	D	SD
20. I feel competent to assist people suffering from trauma.	SA	A	U	D	SD

Please add any comments, especially about your experience of priesthood:

_____

_____

_____

_____

_____

_____

_____

_____

_____

_____

_____

_____

APPENDIX 2

THE 2021 SURVEY COMPOSITE VARIABLES

Adding similar questions together produces composite variables. These combined variables are more reliable and more likely to give a valid reading of the respondents' ideas and feelings.

Composite variables were identified through a principal components analysis and two factor analyses—maximum likelihood and principal axis. These analyses identified groups of individual survey items that could be combined with solid psychometric qualities. In addition, to measure internal consistency or reliability of each of these composite variables, a Cronbach's alpha was computed.

Many of these combined variables included items that had strong face validity to be combined, such as "My morale as a priest is good" and "Overall, I am happy as a priest." One would expect solid psychometric properties for combining these variables, which indeed was the case. The fact that items with strong face value similarity also statistically loaded strongly on the same components suggests that survey respondents took the questions seriously and consistently answered them with integrity.

Survey items were combined simply by adding the two variables together. However, some items needed to be recoded if their Pearson's *r* correlation was negative.

These are the combined variables:

Happiness as a Priest

"My morale as a priest is good."

"Overall, I am happy as a priest."

Cronbach's alpha = .81

Self-Esteem

"I have a good self-image."

"I feel a sense of inner peace."

Cronbach's alpha = .68

Relationship with Bishop

"I have a good relationship with my bishop."

"I support my bishop's leadership."

Cronbach's alpha = .74

Loneliness

"I suffer from loneliness."

"Feeling lonely" (BSI-18 item)

Cronbach's alpha = .80

Sexual Conflicts

"I feel some conflict around my sexuality."

"I know my sexual orientation and I am at peace with it."

Cronbach's alpha =.42

Pearson's r correlation = -.29, $p < .01$

Positive View of Celibacy

"I believe God has called me to live a celibate life."

"Despite its challenges, celibacy has been a grace for me
    personally."

Cronbach's alpha = .85

Traditional Spirituality

"I pray all or most of the Liturgy of the Hours daily."

"I spend time in private prayer daily."

"The Eucharist is the center of my life."

"I have a good relationship with God."

"I feel a sense of closeness to God."

"Mary is an important part of my priestly life."

"I have a devotion to the Blessed Virgin Mary."

"I receive the Sacrament of Penance."

Cronbach's alpha = .77

Relationship with God

"I have a good relationship with God."

"I feel a sense of closeness to God."

Cronbach's alpha = .76

Childhood Trauma

"Growing up, I had a good relationship with my mother."

"Growing up, I had a good relationship with my father."

"I grew up in a dysfunctional family."

"Growing up, I suffered from anxiety and/or depression."

"As a child, I suffered from some trauma."

Cronbach's alpha = .77

Priestly Fraternity

"I have close priest friends."

"Priests in my diocese/religious order are supportive of each other."

"I attend priest gatherings in my diocese/order as often as I can."

Cronbach's alpha = .54

Traumatized by the Crises

"The abuse crisis has negatively impacted my view of the priesthood."

"The abuse crisis has negatively impacted my view of Church leadership."

"The abuse crisis has negatively impacted my faith."

"The COVID-19 pandemic has been traumatic for me personally."

"The abuse crisis has negatively affected my emotional well-being."

"I feel overwhelmed by the COVID-19 pandemic and need more support."

Cronbach's alpha = .80

Priestly Wellness

As noted in the text, this combined variable was formed from adding other combined variables:

Loneliness, Self-Esteem, ProQOL Compassion Satisfaction, Relationship with God, Childhood Trauma, Relationship with Bishop, Priestly Fraternity, Traditional Spirituality, Sexual Conflicts.

Cronbach's alpha = .71

NOTES

Introduction

1. Peter M. J. Stravinskas, "Why Priestly Morale is in the Doldrums," *Catholic World Report*, January 26, 2020, https://www.catholicworldreport.com/2020/01/26/why-priestly-morale-is-in-the-doldrums/.

1. Summary of Findings

1. Mary L. Gautier, Paul M. Perl, and Stephen J. Fichter, *Same Call, Different Men: The Evolution of the Priesthood since Vatican II* (Collegeville, MN: Liturgical Press, 2012), 141.

2. "Cigna Takes Action to Combat the Rise of Loneliness and Improve Mental Wellness in America," Cigna-Newsroom, January 23, 2020, https://newsroom.cigna.com/cigna-takes-action-to-combat-the-rise -of-loneliness-and-improve-mental-wellness-in-america.

3. Nancy L. Sin, Patrick Klaiber, Jin H. Wen, and Anita DeLongis, "Helping amid the Pandemic: Daily Affect and Social Implications of COVID-19-Related Prosocial Activities," *Gerontologist* 61, no. 1 (February 2021): 59–70, https://academic.oup.com/gerontologist/article/61/1/59/5920984?login=false.

2. The Sample and Method of the 2021 Survey

1. See Brad Vermurlen, Stephen Cranney, and Mark Regnerus, *2021 Survey of American Catholic Priests* (*SACP*), https://papers.ssrn.com/sol3/papers.cfm?abstract_id=3951931. It is a confirmation of my data that the mean age in their survey of 1,036 priests was also sixty years old.

3. Priesthood and Happiness

1. Garret Condon, "Priests (Mostly) Happy, Survey Says," *Hartford Courant*, January 19, 2003, https://www.courant.com/news/connecticut/hc-xpm-2003-01-19-0301190010-story.html.

2. Gautier, Perl, and Fichter, *Same Call, Different Men*, 19.

3. Gautier, Perl, and Fichter, *Same Call, Different Men*, 141.

4. Gautier, Perl, and Fichter, *Same Call, Different Men*, 19.

5. Christopher Ingraham, "New Data Shows Americans More Miserable Than We've Been in Half a Century," The Why Axis, January

28, 2022, https://thewhyaxis.substack.com/p/new-data-shows-americans-more-miserable. See also GSS Data Explorer, https://gssdataexplorer.norc.org/trends.

6. John W. Miller, "The Great Resignation and Anti-Work Movement: Catholics Should Celebrate the Changes to Our Labor Market," *America*, February 15, 2022, https://www.americamagazine.org/politics-society/2022/02/15/antiwork-great-resignation-242369.

7. Michelle Boorstein, "The First Christmas as a Layperson: Burned Out by the Pandemic, Many Clergy Quit in the Past Year," *Washington Post*, December 24, 2020, https://www.washingtonpost.com/religion/2021/12/24/christmas-covid-pandemic-clergy-quit/.

8. The subscales Burnout and Secondary Traumatic Stress together constitute one overall measure of Compassion Fatigue.

9. Beth Hudnall Stamm, *The Concise ProQOL Manual*, 2nd ed. (Pocatello, ID: ProQOL.org, 2010), 12, https://img1.wsimg.com/blobby/go/dfc1e1a0-a1db-4456-9391-18746725179b/downloads/ProQOL%20Manual.pdf?ver=1622839353725.

10. "11 Surprising Job Satisfaction Statistics (2022)," Apollo Technical, April 21, 2021, https://www.apollotechnical.com/job-satisfaction-statistics/.

11. Cassidy Rush, "The 25 Most Satisfying Jobs in America," PayScale, June 7, 2017, https://www.payscale.com/career-advice/the-25-most-satisfying-jobs-in-america/.

12. "11 Surprising Job Satisfaction Statistics (2022)."

13. Stephen J. Rossetti, *Why Priests Are Happy: A Study of the Psychological and Spiritual Health of Priests* (Notre Dame, IN: Ave Maria Press, 2011), 94–95.

14. Gautier, Perl, and Fichter, *Same Call, Different Men*, 29–30.

15. Gautier, Perl, and Fichter, *Same Call, Different Men*, 26.

16. National Association of Catholic Theological Schools, "Enter by the Narrow Gate: Satisfaction and Challenges among Recently Ordained Priests," 3, https://cara.georgetown.edu/wp-content/uploads/2020/11/NACTS.pdf.

17. Gautier, Perl, and Fichter, *Same Call, Different Men*, 32.

18. Rossetti, *Why Priests Are Happy*, 88. See also Condon, "Priests (Mostly) Happy, Survey Says."

19. Unusable comments included those that were illegible or were not substantive.

4. Unhappy Priests

1. These two items—"I suffer from loneliness" and the BSI-18 item "feeling lonely"—were strongly mutually correlated at $r = .68$, $p < .001$, and the Cronbach's alpha = .80.

2. Rossetti, *Why Priests Are Happy*, 100. The correlation is slightly different in this source (.33 versus .375) than what is reported because a composite variable was used. However, it essentially measures the same construct.

5. The Mental Health of Priests Today

1. Leonard R. Derogatis, *BSI 18: Administration, Scoring, and Procedures Manual* (Minneapolis, MN: NCS Pearson, 2000), 1.

2. Derogatis, *BSI 18*, 2.

3. Derogatis, *BSI 18*, 6.

4. National Center for Health Statistics, "Anxiety and Depression: Household Pulse Survey," CDC website, https://www.cdc.gov/nchs/covid19/pulse/mental-health.htm. See also Alison Abbott, "Covid's Mental-Health Toll: Scientists Track Surge in Depression," *Nature*, February 11, 2021, https://www.nature.com/articles/d41586-021-00175-z.

5. Carl Bunderson, "Father Danny Roussel of Baton Rouge Remembered as a 'Devoted Priest,'" Catholic News Agency, September 1, 2021, https://www.catholicnewsagency.com/news/248848/father-danny-roussel-of-baton-rouge-remembered-as-a-devoted-priest.

6. Ryan E. Lawrence, Maria A. Oquendo, and Barbara Stanley, "Religion and Suicide Risk: A Systematic Review," *Archives of Suicide Research* 20, no. 1 (2016): 1–21, https://www.ncbi.nlm.nih.gov/pmc/articles/PMC7310534/.

7. Stamm, *The Concise ProQOL Manual*, 12.

8. Rossetti, *Why Priests Are Happy*, 70–71.

9. "Frequently Requested Church Statistics," Center for Applied Research in the Apostolate (CARA), https://cara.georgetown.edu/frequently-requested-church-statistics/.

10. Several survey questions were combined into larger composite variables to strengthen the variables' predictive quality and reliability. There are two questions in the survey that have face validity in

measuring priestly happiness: "My morale as a priest is good" and "Overall, I am happy as a priest." These two questions were combined to form the composite variable Priestly Happiness. (The Cronbach's alpha for these items was .81, which is statistically strong for combining them into a single variable.) Also, the two items "I have a good relationship with my bishop" and "I support my bishop's leadership" were also combined into a single variable, Relationship with Bishop. (The Cronbach's alpha for these two items was .74, which supports combining them together.) Similarly, two items with face validity were combined to form the variable Loneliness: "I suffer from loneliness" and the BSI-18 item "Feeling lonely" (Cronbach's alpha = .80). The variable Inner Peace and Self-Image is a combination of "I have a good self-image" and "I feel a sense of inner peace" (Cronbach's alpha = .73). Finally, Relationship with God is a combination of "I have a good relationship with God" and "I feel a sense of closeness to God" (Cronbach's alpha = .76).

11. For each of the statistics listed, the results were statistically significant at least at the .05 level.

12. Conversely, of the distressed group, 54% strongly agreed or agreed that they suffer from loneliness, while only 4% of the healthy group strongly agreed or agreed.

13. To see if these five items were statistically compatible to form one overall variable, a principal components factor analysis was performed with a varimax rotation. These five variables strongly loaded on one component. Then a Cronbach's alpha test of reliability was performed. The results gave a strong .77, suggesting that they could be thus combined. The intercorrelations of all the variables ranged from .31 to .53.

14. The Cronbach's alpha was .68, and the two items loaded strongly on a single component in the factor analysis.

15. Those who did not suffer from childhood trauma/dysfunction were the upper 25.6% of the scores on the combined Childhood Trauma variable (a score of 24 or 25). Those who did suffer from childhood trauma/dysfunction were the lower 23.4% on the combined Childhood Trauma scale (a score of 6–17).

16. Using post-hoc tests (Tukey and Fisher's LSD), the difference between the newly ordained and the older priests was statistically significant ($p < .05$ or better).

17. Rossetti, *Why Priests Are Happy*, 72–76.

6. Two Crises and Their Effects on Priests

1. Gautier, Perl, and Fichter, *Same Call, Different Men*, 145.

2. Stamm, *The Concise ProQOL Manual*, 13.

3. All correlations cited on this page were statistically significant at $p < .001$ for a two-tailed Pearson's *r* correlation.

4. Nicholaus Garcia, "How's the Boss? Great, according to New Survey," Workforce.com, August 25, 2016, https://www.workforce.com/news/hows-boss-great-according-new-survey.

7. The Relational Lives of Priests

1. The Cronbach's alpha for the two items was .59.

2. Daniel A. Cox, "The State of American Friendship: Change, Challenges, and Loss: Findings from the May 2021 American Perspectives Survey," Survey Center on American Life, June 8, 2021, https://www.americansurveycenter.org/research/the-state-of-american-friendship-change-challenges-and-loss/.

3. "Cigna Takes Action to Combat the Rise of Loneliness."

8. The Spiritual Lives of Priests

1. Brad Vermurlen, Stephen Cranney, and Mark D. Regnerus, "Introducing the 2021 Survey of American Catholic Priests: Overview and Selected Findings," SSRN, November 2, 2021, https://papers.ssrn.com/sol3/papers.cfm?abstract_id=3951931.

2. The Cronbach's alpha for these eight items was a solid .80. Other spirituality items on the survey, such as "I have a spiritual director," that had only a yes/no response, were not combined since they were not continuous variables.

9. Predicting Vulnerability in a Crisis

1. The factor analysis performed was a principal components analysis with the varimax rotation and reporting only those dimensions with an eigenvalue greater than 1. All six items had a factor loading of over .60 on the common dimension. The Cronbach's alpha for these six items was a strong .80. Moreover, combining them into a common dimension had considerable face value as well.

2. The Cronbach's alpha was .54.

3. The Cronbach's alpha for the two items was .68. The Pearson's *r* correlation was .51 ($p < .01$).

4. These five items loaded strongly on a single component in a principal components factor analysis with a varimax rotation and have a solid Cronbach's alpha of .77.

5. These two items loaded strongly on a single component in a principal components factor analysis with a varimax rotation and have Pearson's *r* correlation of -.29 ($p < .01$). There is also strong face validity for combining the two variables.

6. These two items are correlated strongly ($r = .70, p < .01$), and the Cronbach's alpha was .82. So they are statistically able to be combined into a single variable.

10. Why Are Priests Crisis Resilient?

1. Jennifer Guttman, "The Relationship with Yourself: Notes on Self-Confidence and Authenticity," *Psychology Today*, June 27, 2019, https://www.psychologytoday.com/us/blog/sustainable-life-satisfaction/201906/the-relationship-yourself.

2. Sin et al., "Helping amid the Pandemic," 59–70.

3. Gad Levanon et al., "Job Satisfaction 2021," The Conference Board, https://www.conference-board.org/pdfdownload.cfm?masterProductID=27278.

4. Jeanna Bryner, "Survey Reveals Most Satisfying Jobs," *Live Science*, April 17, 2007, https://www.livescience.com/1431-survey-reveals-satisfying-jobs.html.

5. V. J. Felitti et al., "Relationship of Childhood Abuse and Household Dysfunction to Many of the Leading Causes of Death in Adults," *American Journal of Preventive Medicine* 14, no. 4 (May 1998): 245–58.

6. "Adverse Childhood Experiences," National Conference of State Legislatures website, August 23, 2022, https://www.ncsl.org/research/health/adverse-childhood-experiences-aces.aspx.

11. A New Mega Variable: Priest Wellness

1. The variable Priestly Happiness was removed since it is too similar to Wellness in general and thus is not predictive. Interestingly, when removed from these equations, the *r* squared for the regression equations was not greatly reduced since the other variables picked up the slack.

2. All regression equations were significant at $p < .001$.

Postscript: Troubling Trends in America

1. Karen J. Terry et al., *The Causes and Context of Sexual Abuse of Minors by Catholic Priests in the United States, 1950–2010* (Washington, DC: USCCB, 2011), 3, https://www.usccb.org/sites/default/files/issues-and-action/child-and-youth-protection/upload/The-Causes-and-Context-of-Sexual-Abuse-of-Minors-by-Catholic-Priests-in-the-United-States-1950-2010.pdf.

2. Jack Kelly, "More Than Half of U.S. Workers Are Unhappy in Their Jobs," *Forbes*, October 26, 2019, https://www.forbes.com/sites/jackkelly/2019/10/25/more-than-half-of-us-workers-are-unhappy-in-their-jobs-heres-why-and-what-needs-to-be-done-now/?sh=7fab-cdd02024.

3. Holly Hedegaard, Sally Curtin, and Margaret Warner, "Increase in Suicide Mortality in the United States, 1999–2018," NCHS Data Brief No. 362, April 2020, https://www.cdc.gov/nchs/products/databriefs/db362.htm.

4. Jeffrey M. Jones, "U.S. Church Membership Falls below Majority for First Time," Gallup, March 29, 2021, https://news.gallup.com/poll/341963/church-membership-falls-below-majority-first-time.aspx.

5. Ivana Saric, "Poll: 72% of Americans Think U.S. Moving in 'Wrong Direction,'" *Axios*, January 23, 2022, https://www.axios.com/poll-72-america-wrong-direction-54af3071-3f3b-4f2b-a19e-951e63eda522.html.

Msgr. Stephen J. Rossetti, a priest of the Diocese of Syracuse, is an expert on priestly spirituality and wellness issues. He is a Catholic author, speaker, educator, psychologist, and retreat leader. He served for many years at Saint Luke Institute in Maryland, rising to president and CEO.

A graduate of the United States Air Force Academy, Rossetti earned a doctorate in psychology from Boston College and a doctor of ministry degree from the Catholic University of America. Rossetti is the author or editor of twelve books, including *Born of the Eucharist, Letters to My Brothers, The Joy of Priesthood*—recipient of a Catholic Press Association book award—and *Diary of an American Exorcist*. He serves as research associate professor of pastoral studies at the Catholic University of America and is president of St. Michael Center for Spiritual Renewal.

Rossetti received a Proclaim Award from the United States Conference of Catholic Bishops as well as a lifetime service award from the Theological College of the Catholic University of America. In 2010, he earned the Touchstone Award from the National Federation of Priests' Councils for a lifetime of work with priests. In 2013, Rossetti received the Pope John Paul II Seminary Leadership Award from the National Catholic Educational Association for distinguished service in priestly formation and was awarded a doctor of divinity degree, *honoris causa*, from St. Mary's Seminary and University.

ALSO BY
MSGR. STEPHEN J. ROSSETTI

The Joy of Priesthood

Letters to My Brothers
Words of Hope and Challenge
for Priests

The Priestly Blessing
Rediscovering the Gift

Our Journey into Joy
Ten Steps to Priestly Holiness

"Msgr. Stephen J. Rossetti is uniquely qualified
to give sound practical advice to Catholic priests
on how to manage their commitments."
—Avery Cardinal Dulles, SJ